Choctaw

The
Church
and the
Homosexual

The Church

and the

Homosexual

Updated and Expanded Edition

John J. McNeill

Beacon Press   Boston

Beacon Press
25 Beacon Street
Boston, Massachusetts 02108

Beacon Press books
are published under the auspices of
the Unitarian Universalist Association of Congregations.

95 94 93 92 91 90 89 88   8 7 6 5 4 3 2 1

Library of Congress Cataloging-in-Publication Data

McNeill, John J., 1925–
The church and the homosexual.
Bibliography: p.
Includes index.
1. Homosexuality—Religious aspects—Catholic Church.
2. Homosexuality in the Bible.   3. Church work with
homosexuals—United States.   I. Title
HQ76.25.M38   1988   261.8'35766   87-47812
ISBN 0-8070-7901-4

I pray that
with God's merciful grace
this book may serve the spiritual good
of my lesbian sisters and
gay brothers and
all who read it.

Contents

Preface to the New Edition

In his book *The Gentleman From Maryland: The Conscience of a Gay Conservative* (New York: Arbor House, 1986), Robert Bauman speaks of *The Church and the Homosexual* as "a collector's item" because of the difficulty he had in getting his hands on a copy. He praises the book as having brought him hope when he needed it most. I am delighted that with this new updated version, republished by Beacon Press, my book will be easily available once again.

I have paid a high price to make the thought embodied in this book available to the public. Appendix 3 gives the history of the difficulties I encountered in my effort to publish the original edition, difficulties that included my being silenced by the Vatican for nearly ten years on the issue of homosexuality because of this book, my expulsion from the Society of Jesus, and the revocation of my legal right to exercise the priesthood because of my refusal to renounce a public ministry to gay people.

I am aware of hundreds of people who have found peace and self-acceptance in part because of this book. I hope and pray that God will continue to use my work as an instrument of peace and reconciliation for hundreds of others.

Since the original publication of the book, my judgment on several pastoral issues has changed as a result of my continuing work with gay and lesbian clients. These changes primarily concern realistic goals in pastoral counseling, and are discussed in appendix 1.

In addition, AIDS has introduced a whole new dimension to the theological and pastoral issues surrounding homosexual activity, a dimension that was not present twelve years ago when this book was originally written. Some theological and pastoral reflections on the fundamental issues provoked by the AIDS crisis have been added in appendix 2.

A special word of thanks to Josef Dorman, who worked long and hard to keep this book alive and viable, and also to my friend Charles Chiarelli, who spent many long hours proofreading and correcting my manuscripts, and teaching me to use a computer word processor.

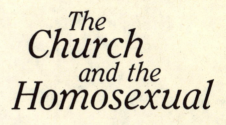

The
Church
and the
Homosexual

Introduction:
The Need for a Reappraisal

The purpose of this introduction is to indicate both the scope and the limits of this moral and pastoral study concerning the homosexual.[1] The first question that must be posed is: What is the need of a reappraisal of the position of traditional moral theology on the question of homosexuality within the Roman Catholic community at this time? That need has become evident in recent years to many Roman Catholic priests and laypersons engaged in pastoral counseling. They have become progressively aware that the two exclusive aims of traditional pastoral counseling—conversion to a heterosexual orientation or total abstinence from all sexual expression—are no longer practical pastoral aims in a majority of the cases with which they deal.[2] Both from their personal experience as counselors and from available scientific evidence they have come to the conclusion that heterosexual adjustment is a practical and successful aim of counseling only in a minority of cases involving basic homosexual psychic orientation. Further, total and unending sexual abstinence attained without severe emo-

tional disorders, and even mental breakdowns, is a practical
and successful goal of counseling again only in a minority of
cases.

The result of adhering to these exclusive goals has been
that many Catholic homosexuals, even a majority, find
themselves faced with a terrible dilemma: either to continue their relationship with the Church at the price of
being cut off from any deep human relationship and deprived of their potentialities for growth and development in
their personal self-identity—not to mention their agonies of
guilt, remorse, self-hatred, and potential emotional breakdown when they fail to achieve the accepted goals—or to
seek their personal growth by means of a homosexual
relationship, only at the price of cutting themselves off from
the Church community and its sacramental life, with all the
attendant guilt and emotional stress which such a separation involves. When a majority of confessors and counselors
find that the traditional guidelines are no longer adequate
but, on the contrary, frequently lead to serious harm and
destruction for their penitents or patients, the need for a
basic critical reexamination of those guidelines should be
obvious.

Not only those engaged in pastoral work and counseling
but the general public as well has come to a new awareness
and a new understanding of the homosexual. In the past the
inadequacies of the traditional ways of dealing with the
homosexual were hidden from the public view by a virtual
conspiracy of silence. Homosexuality was "the sin whose
name should not be mentioned." But, thank God, that
prejudicial silence has been broken. As the Dutch Catechism remarks, it was that silence and the absence of any
open discussion which allowed prejudice and unfounded
fears to flourish, often leading to serious persecutions and
injustices.[3]

A brief summary of some of the articles appearing in Catholic publications in the past few years will help give a clearer idea of this remarkable change. As noted in appendix 3, in 1970 I published a series of three articles entitled "The Christian Male Homosexual" in the July, August, and September issues of the *Homiletic and Pastoral Review*. These articles, resulting from years of counseling experience and scholarly research, proposed a long overdue change in the pastoral approach to the homosexual, designed to correct social injustices and indignities suffered by homosexuals and stressing that they too are children of Christ's redeeming love. The first article attacked stereotypes and popular misunderstandings concerning the homosexual. The second article dealt with the inadequacies of the two traditional pastoral aims in counseling homosexuals—conversion to heterosexuality and total abstinence from all sexual activity. The third article began a process of ethico-moral reevaluation suggesting that perhaps, within their context and under certain circumstances, homosexual relations could be objectively accepted as a lesser evil than promiscuity, etc., and thus be subjectively acceptable to those in such circumstances as morally good. The enthusiastic response from literally hundreds of priests and religious who wrote seeking further information and urging me to do further research and writing in this field made it clear to me that there was a widely felt need for this type of reevaluation.

In 1971 Joseph McCaffrey's article "Homosexuality, Aquinas and the Church" in the *Catholic World* made the point that the Church's attitude toward the homosexual had remained basically the same since Saint Thomas wrote in the twelve hundreds.[4] McCaffrey questioned whether Saint Thomas's understanding of both human nature and human sexuality in general as well as his understanding, or lack thereof, of homosexuality could possibly continue to serve as the basis of moral evaluation today. Father Henry Fahrens, in his article "A Christian Response to Homosexuals" in the September 1972 issue of the *U.S. Catholic*, bore witness from his own and other priests' counseling experience to the inadequacies of the Church's pastoral policies, calling those policies "brutal, self-righteous, prejudicial and un-Christian." Father Fahrens called on the Church to be ready to recognize homosexual relations and went so far as to recommend "a witness of the Church to the celebration of love between two people of the same sex."

Commonweal was the next Catholic publication to turn to the issue of homosexuality. The 6 April 1973 issue devoted two major articles and an editorial to the question. The editorial urged the Church to support civil rights legislation for the homosexual and observed that "some Catholic moralists have cautiously argued in professional journals that under certain circumstances which may differ with each individual a Catholic homosexual can enter an active homosexual relationship and still receive the sacraments and lead a life of sexual love which does not necessarily separate him from the love of God."[5] Tom Driver, in his article "Homosexuality: The Contemporary and Christian Contexts," takes the position that appears to be quite generally accepted among Protestant moralists, namely, that "the forms of sexual love do not matter when compared to the dignity of persons and their capacity for trust and love." The gay liberation movement, Driver contends, has raised homosexuality to the level of political consciousness. As a result, we can no longer deal with it as if it were merely a psychological problem or a question of private morality; rather, it is now a question of public policy. "The movement should have our thanks if it causes us to reconsider the policies of marriage, and most of all, if it helps us to see that sexual plurality is the very scene and stage upon which are played out the dramas of love."

Peter Fink, S.J., in the same issue proposed what he called "A Pastoral Hypothesis." He points out that pastoral activity cannot be left in abeyance until complex theological questions are resolved with total clarity. In fact, pastoral activity itself is the source of essential data needed for theological reflection. Fink's hypothesis is that the Church should explore the possibility that homosexual love is a valid form of human love, and, consequently, can also mediate God's loving presence. In the absence of any definitive condemnation of all homosexual activity a priori, it is a valid theological method, Fink argues, to explore this hypothesis and judge its validity on the basis of its consequences. "If homosexual love is sinful this will show itself as destructive of the human and disruptive of man's relation with God." In counseling, the Church should take the gay and lesbian couple and their attempt at a love union with radical seriousness. "All I ask here is that the Church employ all its resources in an honest effort to lead gay people to love, to the human and to God *through* their homosexuality."

Over Labor Day weekend in 1973 the first national convention of Dignity was held in Los Angeles. I was invited to be the keynote speaker. In my speech I summarized all the evidence in favor of a moral reevaluation of homosexual relations. In its 5 October 1973 issue the *National Catholic Reporter* published my speech and commented in its editorial that there is a growing evidence that it is time for the Church to re-examine its attitude toward the homosexual.[6] What is needed, according to the editor, is "that the Church, individually and corporately, publicly and privately, should sit down with homosexuals and talk in an atmosphere characterized by enlightenment and compassion, not ignorance and invective."

The next major publication occurred again in *Commonweal*. In the 15 February 1974 issue, Gregory Baum in his article "Catholic Homosexuals" saw the affirmation of gay Catholicism in the form of their organization Dignity as raising many theological questions. The first has to do with the argument traditionally brought against homosexual activity, that based on so-called human nature. We are much more aware today that what was accepted in the past as human nature is a human creation and frequently contains dehumanizing elements which call for theological criticism. Are the prohibitions against homosexuality, Baum asks, "a legitimation of the inherited social structures which assign men and women definitive and unequal places?" Theologians seeing the collective crimes and violence inflicted on homosexual men and women begin to suspect that the traditional arguments against homosexuality are based not so much on a sound concept of nature as on a refusal to take a close look at the foundations of our culture. The crucial moral question, Baum feels, is whether homosexuality is open to mutuality. Is the homosexual orientation capable of grounding friendship that enables the partners to grow and become more human? If the answer is yes, then the task of Catholic homosexuals is to acknowledge themselves as such before God, accept their sexual inclination as an aspect of their calling, and explore the meaning of this inclination for Christian life. This, Baum claims, is the position adopted by Dignity. Dignity holds that it is the call of the Catholic homosexual to affirm his or her sexual orientation in faith, to regard themselves as equal members of the believing community, and to express their sexuality in a manner consonant with Christ's teaching of love.

Homosexual men and women, Baum claims, are in greater need of self-knowledge and personal wisdom than other people. In our culture gay people are often the wounded, and they must wrestle with themselves before the freedom to love and to forgive themselves becomes accessible to them. But to whom are they to go? If gay people will ever find guidelines to heal themselves of the wounds that lead to hostility and self-hatred, it will be a wisdom generated within the homosexual community itself. Dignity trusts that the guidance granted by the Spirit within the Christian community will lead to greater insight into unresolved questions. Baum believes it is not likely that the Catholic Church is about to change its traditional teaching, namely, that all homosexual activity, no matter what the circumstances, is sinful. Therefore he thought it would be a mistake for Dignity to make an appeal to the Catholic hierarchy for special recognition. Rather, Baum proposes what he terms a realistic strategy: "to create a moderate and well-founded minority position in the Catholic Church which would be a help to vast numbers of gay people at this time, collect more pastoral experience and continue theological reflection."

Gregory Baum's prediction proved prophetic. Dignity's letter addressed to the bishops of the United States from its first national convention, appealing for dialogue, went unheeded for the most part. In its place the Bishops' Committee on Pastoral Research and Practice issued a fifteen-page article: "Principles to Guide Confessors in Questions of Homosexuality." The principles enunciated in the guidelines are basically a repetition of the Church's traditional stand concerning homosexuality. Homosexuality is seen as contrary not only to the procreative purpose of human sexuality, "but also to the other principle, which is to express mutual love between husband and wife." The guidelines also claim that homosexual activity is clearly condemned in Scripture, especially in Paul's Epistle to the Romans. The document summarizes various theories as to the cause of homosexuality, with the presumption that it represents a pathological condition. Despite its obvious limitations, some writers praised the guidelines as the first document originating from Church authorities in recent times to give explicit attention to the homosexual question. The most important new element in the text is the encouragement of sexually nonactive homosexual friendships. Traditionally many moralists argued that homosexuals should avoid such friendships because they could be an "occasion of sin." However, the bishops' statement argues that "other elements in his [the homosexual's] plan of life and spiritual direction can temper this danger which is justified considering his need for deep human relationships, and the good which will come from them in the future." However, the document insists, if a homosexual friendship begins to involve regular overt sexual activity, then the homosexual must be admonished to break off the relationship, with the sanction for refusal to do so the refusal of absolution.

The primary source of the bishops' guidelines is to be found in the writings of John Harvey.[7] Father Harvey is a pioneer in the area of moral studies and research concerning homosexuality. He takes a strongly negative view of homosexual relationships, believing them to be contrary to God's will as revealed in Scripture and, from his own pastoral experience, humanly destructive. Father Harvey has sought the financial assistance of the American bishops to open an institution for homosexual priests where they could receive special psychological and spiritual assistance.

At its annual meeting in Denver in 1972, the National Federation of Priests' Councils passed a resolution dealing with ministry to the homosexual community. The Federation noted that "the Church's concern for and ministry to the homosexual community is practically invisible and, therefore, nonexistent in the United States." Consequently, the Federation voted to establish a task force to develop a model for a Christian ministry to the homosexual community. That model was developed by a gay ministry task force which the Justice and Peace Commission of the Salvatorian

Fathers established in 1972. A thirty-eight-page set of guidelines, entitled "A Model for Ministry to the Homosexual Community," was presented to the Executive Committee of the National Federation of Priests' Councils to be submitted to the delegates for a vote in the 1974 national convention. The guidelines called for full participation of homosexuals in the Eucharist and directed that confessions of homosexuals who have accepted their condition and are comfortable with it should not center on the fact of homosexuality but on whether the individual is living up to "the demands of the Christian faith and conversion *as a homosexual.*"

At that convention the Executive Board of the National Federation refused to present the guidelines for a vote by the membership on the grounds that they were "not complete enough." President Reid Mayo referred to a report by Charles Curran to the effect that the guidelines made the assumption that "there is nothing wrong with homosexual acts per se and that there is no difference between homosexuality and heterosexuality." Curran felt that many theological issues which still remained to be decided among theologians were assumed resolved in the guidelines. Consequently, in place of a vote on the guidelines, the National Federation of Priests' Councils voted unanimously for "a development of the theology of homosexuality." This book is conceived precisely as an effort to make a contribution to that development.

Another circumstance which calls for a reappraisal of the traditional moral position of the Church is the fact that the homosexual community itself has evolved a new self-awareness and a new militancy. Homosexuals in large numbers are no longer content to suffer prejudice and injustice passively; they have grouped together and formed organizations to promote their own sense of self-pride and heal the deep wounds left by their status as a persecuted minority, as well as to promote their own legal and political rights. Perhaps for the first time in history self-accepting homosexuals have emerged as a political force.

This new self-awareness and militancy is not limited, however, to the social and political order; there is a new consciousness and a new militancy among believing gay men and lesbian women who are active members of the various churches. The emergence of the Metropolitan Community Church as an interim Christian community for those homosexuals who are not accepted in the other churches is an example of this. Homosexuals from other churches have begun to group together in organizations such as Dignity (Catholic), Integrity (Episcopalian), Acceptance (Methodist), Lutherans Concerned, Evangelicals Concerned, etc. These homosexuals wish to remain faithful and actively participating members of their Church. But they will no longer accept without challenge the Church's traditional teaching and practice in their regard. They insist on being dealt with as a group, and no longer as isolated individuals; they insist on their right to be represented and to contribute from their collective knowledge and experience to a reappraisal of the Church's traditional pastoral treatment of them. They are anxious to contribute to the task of separating the wheat from the chaff; that is, the real implications of Christian faith and morals concerning their life-style from the traditional customs and prejudices which, as they see it, an often all-too-human heterosexual Church community has imposed on them. For they feel that this Church tradition owes its origin more to prejudice and misunderstanding than to the true implications of Christian faith.

The Church's traditional pastoral position concerning homosexuals was, however, by no means a purely arbitrary stance. It had its foundation in the Church's understanding of the sources of revelation, both Scripture and tradition, and in the traditional interpretation of these sources insofar as they can contribute to the formation of a theological understanding of human sexuality. It had its foundation also in the "natural law" tradition of moral philosophy and moral theology espoused by the Church. Consequently, the Church cannot in good conscience change its pastoral position in such a way that its practice would be in violation of its understanding of both revelation and theology.

The magisterium's pronouncement dealing with homosexuality, issued by the Sacred Congregation for the Doctrine of the Faith on 15 January 1976 and entitled "Declaration on Certain Questions Concerning Sexual Ethics," is to my knowledge the first official Church document which deals, among other questions, with the pastoral and moral issues concerning homosexuality. The Declaration is an important document of serious ecclesiastical authority and, as such, it merits a respectful and serious hearing on the part of all who recognize that authority. Although the Declaration is an authoritative pronouncement on what the official teaching of the institutional Church is, it is not, however, an infallible teaching. Its importance is based on extrinsic authority rather than intrinsic argument. There is no effort to present evidence, nor is there any indication of sources, but only a series of authoritative declarations. Consequently it does not simply close the door to all further discussion of the question on the part of competent scholars in the manner of competent scholarship.

Dealing with the moral questions concerning homosexuality, the Declaration speaks of those "who, basing themselves on observations in the psychological order, have begun to judge indulgently, or even to excuse completely, homosexual relations between certain people." The Declaration is the first Church document to grant the legitimacy of the distinction—so important, as we shall see, for moral evaluation—between those who indulge in homosexual activities and those who share in a permanent homosexual condition. Although it grants the validity of the distinction, it does not explore its implications for moral judgment. The document accepts the opinion, rejected by the American Psychiatric Association, that a permanent homosexual psychological condition is "pathological."

In regard to constitutional homosexuals, the document notes: "Some people conclude that their tendency is so natural that it justifies in their case homosexual relations within a sincere communion of life and love analogous to marriage insofar as such homosexuals feel incapable of enduring a solitary life." It then goes on to insist on pastoral compassion and understanding in dealing with such homosexuals: "[They] must be treated with understanding and sustained in the hope of overcoming their personal difficulties and their inability to fit into society." Further, because "in sins of the sexual order . . . it more easily happens that free consent is not fully given," the document calls for "prudence" in judging culpability of homosexuals. However, the Declaration is quite clear that "no pastoral method can be employed which would give moral justification to these acts on grounds that they would be consonant with the condition of such people."

Consequently, the authors of the Declaration find themselves in the dilemma of denying the pastor what, in the opinion of many, would be the only realistic means of truly helping the homosexual to overcome his or her difficulty and to fit into society. As the editors of the *Tablet*, the Catholic newspaper of the Brooklyn diocese, noted in the issue of 22 January 1976:

> To recommend overcoming the incurable is to counsel the impossible, and it is precisely because of the frustration of such a situation that moral theologians are exploring other pastoral solutions. The pastoral sensitivity recommended by the Declaration might lead to

an understanding ministry to such persons, but there must also be some deeper inquiry into the nature of the moral condition itself.

Why do the authors of the Declaration place themselves in this dilemma? They make quite clear in the Declaration that they do not see their pastoral conclusion as arbitrary; rather, they see it as necessitated by their understanding of sacred Scripture and of tradition. In sacred Scripture, the document states, "they [homosexual relations] are condemned as a serious depravity and even presented as the sad consequence of rejecting God." The document does note that Scripture does not permit us to conclude that all those who are homosexuals are personally responsible. However, it nevertheless concludes that the Scriptures "attest to the fact that homosexual acts are intrinsically disordered and can in no way be approved of."

The second argument is based on a certain understanding of moral philosophy and theology, namely that all homosexual acts in the objective moral order "lack an essential and indispensable finality." The basic question here is one of understanding what is the God-given nature and meaning of human sexuality as such. The Church has traditionally held that the only context which can give moral meaning to human sexuality according to God's will is "a relationship which realizes the full sense of mutual self-giving and human procreation in the context of true love."

I am fully in sympathy with the Congregation's concern to preserve moral and human values in the realm of human sexuality. The Church must carry out its divinely appointed task of searching out the context in which human sexual activity is conformed to the will of God and the spirit of Christ. Further, I remind my readers once again that I am not the magisterium; nor do I have the authority to speak in the name of the Church. However, I can speak on this subject with some authority. I am a qualified and accredited theologian and an expert in the field of sexual ethics. I have spent many years studying, counseling, and working with the Catholic homosexual community. My opinions have been shared with my colleagues and revised to meet their legitimate criticisms. The value of what I have to say is not based on extrinsic authority but on the value of the reasoning and evidence that I can bring to bear.

It is my opinion, which I will try to demonstrate in this book, that the limitations on pastoral practice imposed once again by the Declaration will be destructive of the values the document wishes to preserve and will continue to prove humanly destructive of the majority of Catholic homosexuals who attempt to live according to its directives. In the words, once again, of the editors of the *Tablet:* "We are deeply committed to the right and duty of ecclesiastical authority to teach the truth, but not to the presumption that ecclesiastical authority can create the truth."

Consequently, the Declaration makes quite clear that before there can be any authentic change in pastoral practice, there must first be a critical reappraisal of the sources of traditional practice both in moral philosophy and moral theology. Such a critical reappraisal becomes even more necessary and urgent in the light of the new methodologies in both biblical studies and moral theology and new data arising especially from the human sciences such as psychology and sociology. By applying the new methodologies and taking into consideration the new data, many moral theologians have come to the conclusion that many of the basic certitudes of the past which served as the foundation and justification of pastoral practice regarding homosexuality can and should be open to critical reexamination.

First of all there is an urgent need to apply the new methodologies of biblical scholarship to scriptural data.

The primary source of the traditional condemnation of homosexual activity as contrary to the divine will has been the interpretation of certain texts both in the Old and New Testaments which have been understood as dealing with this subject. Unfortunately, in using Scripture to deal with homosexuality many still use a text-picking approach, but biblical scholarship has advanced beyond this approach in most other areas. There is general recognition that to get at the true message of Scripture one must use advanced linguistic tools; one must consider individual texts in their larger context; one must also consider the cultural and historical circumstances of the time. As a result, a new understanding of the biblical treatment of human sexuality in general seems to be emerging among biblical scholars; they appear to be moving toward the realization that Scripture does indeed teach a "personalist" understanding of human sexuality over against the legalist tradition based in natural law.

As I note in this study, there has been surprisingly little scholarly biblical work dealing with homosexuality. However, I have attempted to gather together the results of such studies as have been made. These studies tend to cast serious doubt on the claim that one can find a clear condemnation of all homosexual activity as such, independent of circumstances, in Scripture, or that one can find a clear revelation of God's will which is applicable to the situation of most homosexuals as we understand the situation today.

With regard to the treatment of the biblical material, a special word of gratitude should go to Dr. John Boswell of Yale University. It was while reading his brilliant scholarly reflections, subsequently published in *Christianity, Social Tolerance, and Homosexuality* (Chicago and London: University of Chicago Press, 1980), dealing with the loci in the epistles of Saint Paul supposedly concerned with homosexuality, that I first became aware that the traditional scriptural

basis for the condemnation of homosexual acts as contrary
to the revealed will of God was open to serious question.
A special debt of gratitude is due also to D. Sherwin
Bailey, whose classic work *Homosexuality in the Western
Christian Tradition* still remains the outstanding scholarly work on the subject. I have drawn heavily upon it.
Bailey's treatment of the Old Testament passages, especially the Sodom and Gomorrah story in Genesis, first
opened my eyes to the fact that the sin of Sodom and
Gomorrah was understood by many biblical scholars to
be not homosexuality but inhospitality to the stranger.
Peter Ellis's book *The Yahwist: The Bible's First Theologian* provided essential information on the Yahwist's
persistent theme of ridiculing pagan fertility worship,
which helps to put the sexual elements of the Sodom and
Gomorrah story into perspective. John McKenzie's book
The World of the Judges threw light on the parallel
passage, the Crime of Gibeah, in Judges. T. C. DeKruijf's
The Bible on Sexuality provided me with a key to the
understanding of the difference in the treatment of human sexuality in the Old and New Testaments. And
finally a special word of thanks belongs to Herman van de
Spijker, whose work *Die Gleichgeschlechtliche Zuneigung* provided a basically confirmatory analysis of biblical passages.

Also I wish to thank the two biblical scholars who took
the time to read over and criticize my manuscript and
give me the help of their specialized knowledge. The
first, who prefers to remain unnamed, gave me invaluable
help with the Old Testament materials. The second,
Father William G. Thompson, S.J., whose special studies
on the Pauline aspects of the question made him a
particularly competent reader, gave me important support in my confrontation with critics. I would like to
quote from his critical report:

I find your treatment of the biblical data judicious and responsible. You clearly disclaim credentials as a biblical scholar and state your dependence on the work of specialists. But within that limitation your selection and arrangement of materials is well-ordered and clear. You obviously have a sense of how an argument from Scripture about a current issue is to be developed. . . . Concerning methodological issues I could not agree more with your assessment of the impact of recent biblical studies in the Church on both dogmatic positions and moral/pastoral questions. . . . Consensus among theologians is not a matter of counting heads. It is a question of those who have understood and made operative in their theology the developments in biblical studies and those who have not.

I make no pretense to be a biblical scholar; I have attempted to gather together the results of the best scholarship concerning those passages in the Old and New Testaments traditionally understood as dealing with homosexuality. My hope is that this summary treatment I give the subject may inspire qualified biblical scholars to undertake a much more thorough study.

When we look at tradition, we find that tradition in turn relies both on a questionable use of Scripture and on a relatively unexamined cultural inheritance. The only new element which enters the picture is the use of "natural law" tradition in scholastic philosophy to buttress the conclusions originally derived from Scripture and cultural practice. As in many other areas of moral philosophy, the advances made in philosophical anthropology, where the human is understood along dynamic lines of self-creative freedom rather than static essence, serve as a basis for a critical reexamination of the traditional condemnation of homosexuality derived from the natural law approach of the Scholastics. We are much more aware today of the extent to which human sexual orientation is the result of a free cultural adaptation rather than biological instinct. The emphasis in ethics concerns a search for ideal goals which should serve as guide and norm for that free cultural development. Sexual ethics in general places a much greater stress on the interpersonal dimension as the proper context within which sexual behavior can be and must be ethically evaluated. Greater stress must be placed on the actual situation of the parties involved. Once all these factors are taken into consideration, the traditional treatment of homosexuality in philosophical ethics appears seriously inadequate.

To avoid possible misunderstandings I would like to call to the attention of my readers the philosophical background from which I approach moral issues in general and sexual morality in particular. It will become evident quickly to the discerning reader that I am not following the classical "natural law" philosophy. Rather, I consider myself a disciple of the great French Catholic philosopher Maurice Blondel, whose philosophy of action was one of the principal sources of Teilhard de Chardin's thought and played an essential role in the thinking of many of the periti at the Second Vatican Council.

In my book *The Blondelian Synthesis,* I discussed Blondel's fundamental personalist framework for moral evaluation in the chapter entitled "The Problem of Interpersonality."[8] I evolved a Blondelian methodology for moral decision making in a paper entitled "Necessary Structures of Freedom," presented to the Jesuit Philosophical Association,[9] and again from a different perspective in my paper entitled "Freedom of Conscience in Theological Perspective," presented to a pastoral psychology symposium at Fordham University in 1971.[10] I further developed my ideas on freedom, person, and nature in an article in a special *Theological Studies* issue on moral problems in genetics: "Human Freedom and the Future."[11] Finally, I applied that methodology and its insights to sexual morality in general in a two-part article, "Joseph Fletcher on Sexual Behavior: A Critical Comment," in the April and May 1969 issues of the *Homiletic and Pastoral Review*.[12]

There have also been significant changes in the approach of moral theology to sexual ethics in general. Under the influence of recent psychological insights there has been a movement away from the act-centered methodology of the past toward an orientation-centered methodology. As O'Neil and Donovan note in their book *Sexuality and Moral Responsibility*, the moral quality of sexual activity cannot be judged from the isolated act; rather it involves "a responsible orientation toward growth and reconciliation."[13] Therefore, the question must be posed: Can homosexual activities within the context of a homosexual interpersonal relationship represent a responsible orientation toward growth and reconciliation? Another change which must be taken into consideration is the recent emphasis on the coequality of the ends of sexuality, procreation and mutual support and fulfillment. As long as procreation was held as the primary aim of all legitimate sexual activity, it was relatively easy to condemn homosexual activity, since it necessarily contradicted that primary aim. It is interesting to note that during the birth-control controversy many traditional moralists resisted any effort to challenge that primacy on the grounds that it would tend to undermine the Church's traditional position concerning homosexual activities. The question must now be posed: If a homosexual relationship can achieve the coequal aim of mutual support and fulfillment, is it morally acceptable?[14]

Once again, there certainly is a need for a definitive work on the development of the Church's tradition concerning homosexuality, a work along the lines of Noonan's classical study of contraception and Callahan's study of abortion.

The best that can be done in this book is to point out those aspects of tradition concerning homosexuality which are open to critical reexamination owing to the various changes we have noted. It is my hope, once again, that this study may inspire competent scholars to undertake such a work.

Finally, we must consider the enormous amount of new, significant data derived from the human sciences such as psychology, psychiatry, sociology, anthropology, and comparative cultural studies. These data have provided the moralist with an understanding of human sexuality—its etiology, development, cultural dependency, etc.—which calls into question many of the implicit assumptions of the past. One factor which tends to confirm moral theologians in upholding the traditional condemnation of homosexuality is the position of a prevalent school of psychiatrists that homosexuality is an abnormal form of sexual development and constitutes mental illness. However, many prominent psychiatrists have recently challenged their colleagues on this point. In fact, by a unanimous decision the trustees of the American Psychiatric Association have voted to remove homosexuality from the list of mental illnesses, and a majority vote of the membership upheld that decision of the board of trustees. Contrary to traditional belief, several recent studies have revealed the presence in society of many healthy, well-adjusted, and productive people living in stable and happy homosexual relationships. The presence of these relatively happy and whole people in stable relationships that are homosexual exposes the weak epistemological basis of much previous moral evaluation, since it was based on incomplete and inaccurate data.[15]

All efforts in the past to establish a definitive etiological explanation of homosexuality in terms of either constitutional or environmental factors have run into serious difficulties. The result has been controversy and disagreement among psychologists and psychiatrists concerning the etiology, status in terms of mental health, and proper treatment for homosexuals. Some moralists have tended to accept the disputed conclusions of one or another school of psychologists and psychiatrists. Still others have manifested a tendency to make an unjustified transition from supposed psychological data to a moral conclusion. Because, for example, homosexuals were supposedly deprived of proper parental relations in early childhood (psychological), therefore they must work to overcome their homosexuality and become heterosexual (moral). I have attempted to summarize these recent developments in psychology and psychiatry which call into question the traditional theories concerning homosexuality. I have also critically examined the moral implications of certain methods of treatment, as well as some of the false transitions from psychological theory to moral judgment.

In their traditional presentation of moral obligation, Aquinas and Alphonsus Liguori, among others, always maintained *nulla obligatio imponatur nisi sit certa.* Given, as I believe, (1) the uncertainty of clear scriptural prohibition, (2) the questionable basis of the traditional condemnation in moral philosophy and moral theology, (3) the emergence of new data which upset many traditional assumptions, and (4) controversies among psychologists and psychiatrists concerning theory, etiology, treatment, and so on, there obviously is a need to open up anew the question of the moral standing of homosexual activity and homosexual relationships for public debate. Further, this debate must be public and cannot be limited to a peer-group discussion by experts, because the empirical experience of the Catholic homosexual community is a most important and even essential contribution for a successful outcome of that debate.

To anticipate for a moment the conclusion I will draw at the end of this work, it would appear to follow that the same

moral rules apply to homosexual as to heterosexual attitudes and behavior. Those that are responsible, respectful,
loving, and truly promotive of the good of both parties are
moral; those that are exploitive, irresponsible, disrespect-
ful, or destructive of the true good of either party must be
judged immoral. I am aware that this conclusion moves
beyond the position reached by many of my fellow theologians and the present teaching of the official magisterium.
Some moralists, for example, insist that the connection
between human sexuality and procreation is clearly established in Scripture. To quote one expert:

> In succinct form the biblical norm for human sexuality
> is this: man and woman joined together in one flesh in
> faithful love . . . specifically, the bind I feel is not lo-
> cated in the Christian norm itself. Theologically I sub-
> scribe to that norm with conviction. For me the prob-
> lem lies in how the norm is used in Church and
> society; what is done by design or default to those who
> violate it. The homosexual bears pressures, indignities
> and injustices which demand relief. The question is
> how to take up his cause without either sacrificing the
> norm or sanctioning its use as a cover for persecution.

In the ongoing dialogue with this man and other moral
theologians, the primary and most fundamental criticism I
have received is that in attempting to discover a genuinely
helpful pastoral approach I have come close to losing hold
on that so-called biblical norm. Consequently, they claim
that the burden of proof is on me to show that the man-
woman relationship as traditionally understood in our culture is not "biblically and anthropologically normative."
The entire first section of this book attempts to respond to
that objection. I leave to the reader to decide whether or not
I have adequately responded.

Another objection to my position arises from the belief of many moralists that the procreative framework provides the only valid ground for rational moral judgment and the only real corrective in society to hedonistic selfishness. Thus it is held that any moral approval of homosexual activity could result in a fundamental moral breakdown affecting the whole human community. As one critic suggests, my treatment of homosexuality implicitly opens up, but does not attempt to resolve, a host of other questions concerning sexual morality—such as premarital sex and extramarital sex—by challenging the marriage-and-procreation framework within which these questions have traditionally been resolved. In response to this objection I believe it is important, first of all, to grasp realistically the fact that owing to many factors—longer life-span, overpopulation, birth control, the women's movement, the development of asexual means of procreation, and so on—the procreative context is necessarily breaking down and factually will no longer serve in the future as a practical means of regulating and judging the moral worth of the greater part of human sexual activity. Further, I believe that the interpersonal context properly understood (which is also a biblically approved, normative context) can and will provide an adequate framework for moral judgment and healthy regulation of human sexual activity both in heterosexual and in homosexual relationships. In this respect the emergence of a visible homosexual community both in society and in the Church can be seen as providential, because the homosexual community must perforce learn to deal with human sexuality outside the context of procreation. Their own happiness and human fulfillment demand that they find in the framework of interpersonal relationships those forms of sexual expression which can be healthy and conducive to growth. In searching out this framework, the homosexual community could supply the entire human community with irreplaceable empirical evidence on how sexual morality and sexual mores must change in the future.

There is still another set of criticisms to which I would like to respond briefly. Some readers of my manuscript have thought that my treatment of this subject is too partisan. They see me as a proponent of "advocacy theology," giving a strong bias to one side of the question. These readers seem to miss the point that almost everything that has been written in the past in moral theology concerning homosexuality has been "advocacy theology" biased in a negative direction. I leave to the reader the judgment of whether or not my treatment is biased. For my part, I did my best to present fairly all the evidence for and against each thesis I dealt with. I never deliberately omitted or distorted any evidence, even though it was contrary to my convictions. However, even if there is an element of truth in this criticism, I would still feel justified in my approach. For too long all we have seen is writing and counseling biased in the other direction. One of my goals is to open up a new dialogue by pushing the dialogical pendulum a bit in the opposite direction.

This reappraisal opens up the possibility of a new dimension to the theological evaluation of homosexuality. If homosexuality is not necessarily contrary to nature and the divine will, then the question may be posed: For what purpose does the homosexual exist? What positive contribution can the homosexual make to the human community as such? The second part of this study explores this teleological aspect of homosexuality. It is my deepest conviction that only by trying to respond to these questions can the moral theologian deal adequately with the human phenomenon of homosexuality; only thus can a positive understanding of that phenomenon be achieved, an understanding which can effectively destroy the grounds of prejudice, injustice, and persecution and liberate homosexual men and women to make a positive contribution to the development of a more human community.

After summarizing the various grounds for a reevaluation of homosexuality from the viewpoint of moral theology in part 1 of this study, and exploring the positive contribution that the homosexual community can make to human development in part 2, I attempt in part 3 to explore in outline the implications for pastoral practice in terms of both individual counseling and institutional policy. The Christians who without any fault of their own share the homosexual condition are a very real factor in our midst. Perhaps no single group of human beings has been subjected to greater injustice, persecution, and suffering than they. And, even if inculpably, the Church shares a heavy burden of responsibility for this situation. The single purpose which has inspired this study has been to make some effort to understand the special problem that faces gays and lesbians who wish to remain in the Church and to offer practical and responsible solutions to the dilemma they face, solutions compatible with our present state of knowledge and with the deepest implications of Christian faith and morality.

I am particularly indebted to Charles Curran for providing the inspiration especially for the first part of this study. His book *Catholic Moral Theology in Dialogue* contains a chapter, entitled "Dialogue with the Homophile Movement: The Morality of Homosexuality," in which he outlines the methodological and substantive considerations which must enter into moral theology's evaluation of homosexuality. While agreeing for the most part with his methodology, I have found it necessary on several occasions to respectfully disagree with his conclusions. A critical reflection on Curran's chapter convinced me that I should attempt to put into writing the experience and the various criticisms which have occurred to me over the years, since the publication of my article "The Christian Male Homosexual" in the *Homiletic and Pastoral Review*.

Part 1

1

Moral Theology and Homosexuality

The Present Situation

The chapter entitled "Dialogue with the Homophile Movement: The Morality of Homosexuality" in Father Curran's book *Catholic Moral Theology in Dialogue*[1] represents an important contribution, made by an outstanding professional moral theologian in the Catholic Church, to a serious reconsideration of the Church's attitude toward the homosexual. Father Curran's position merits serious consideration by the Catholic homophile community in order to discern both the advanced understanding of their situation that it manifests and the limits of that understanding, and especially the value of the reasoning Father Curran advances in defense of those limits.

Although he finds himself in disagreement with the reasoning I employed in my earlier article, "The Christian Male Homosexual" in the *Homiletic and Pastoral Review*,[2] as he understands it, Curran says he finds himself "in general agreement with the practical conclusions proposed by McNeill." In his own words, he summarizes these conclusions as follows:

29

The homosexual is generally not responsible for his condition. . . . Therapy, as an attempt to make the homosexual into a heterosexual, does not offer great promise for most homosexuals. Celibacy and sublimation are not always possible or even desirable for the homosexual. There are many somewhat stable homosexual unions which afford their partners some human fulfillment and contentment. Obviously such unions are better than homosexual promiscuity . . . the individual homosexual may morally come to the conclusion that a somewhat permanent homosexual union is the best, and sometimes the only, way for him to achieve some humanity. Homosexuality can never became an ideal. Attempts should be made to overcome this condition if possible; however, at times one may reluctantly accept homosexual unions as the only way in which some people can find a satisfying degree of humanity in their lives.[3]

I will discuss further the respects in which my own conclusions differ from those of Curran. But the point I would like to make at the beginning is that these practical conclusions which Curran accepts represent a substantial advance over the traditional position in Catholic moral theology, which tended in the past to see all homosexual relations as subjectively and objectively mortally sinful and thus left the Catholic homosexual no morally acceptable alternative except a life of total abstinence from sexual activity. In practice these conclusions imply that under certain conditions a Catholic homosexual can enter into an active homosexual relationship and still receive the sacraments and live a life of sexual love which does not necessarily separate him or her from the love of God in Christ.

What are the limits, however, which Curran finds necessary to place on the Church's moral acceptance of homosex-

uality? He speaks of his theory as a "theory of compromise":

> In the theory of compromise, the particular action [ho-
> mosexual] in one sense is not objectively wrong be-
> cause in the presence of sin it remains the only viable
> alternative for the individual. However, in another
> sense the action is wrong and manifests the power of
> sin. If possible, man must try to overcome sin, but the
> Christian knows that the struggle against sin is never
> totally successful in this world.[4]

These limitations carry with them the logical implication
that while Catholic homosexuals may be morally justified in
entering into a homosexual relationship temporarily, owing
to their objectively sinful condition, they must continue to
do everything in their power to free themselves from their
need of that relationship, since it represents the power of
sin over them.

At the beginning of his article Curran acknowledges that
a moral study should not be done independent of its
relation to pastoral practice. "This study should, however,
furnish a basis for forming a proper pastoral approach to the
homosexual and the homophile community . . . ."[5] At the
end of the article he reverts to the pastoral implications of
his moral theory by conceding: "One can object that such
a view still relegates the homosexual to second-class
citizenship."[6] But, he responds, "one can still love and
respect the person even though one believes his homosexual behavior falls short of the full meaning of human
sexuality. In many other areas of life I can judge a person's
behavior as being wrong or less than ideal and still respect
him as a person."[7] Curran probably has in mind here the
objection on the part of Catholic homosexuals against the
tendency of many priests to pass objective moralistic judg-

ments that render their pastoral counseling ineffective. I
believe he misses the point of the objection. The problem is
not the ability of the confessor or counselor to pass judgment on the homosexual condition as an objective manifes-
tation of sin, whatever may be the truth of that judgment,
while still respecting the individual as person. The problem, rather, is the homosexual's consequent judgment on
himself, or herself, if the judgment that the homosexual
condition is objectively sinful is uncritically accepted by
the person in question.[8]

How can Christian homosexuals accept themselves and
their homosexuality with any sense of their own dignity and
value as long as they must see themselves and their actions
as organically expressing the effects of sin in the world and
as essentially in contradiction to the divine will for man?
How can individuals with such an understanding of themselves possibly enter into a constructive homosexual relationship which expresses true human love? Curran's position calls to mind an article by Joseph Epstein in *Harper's
Magazine*.[9] While professing many liberal attitudes toward
the homosexual, Epstein concludes his article by compar-
ing him to the leper of Old Testament times. Epstein's
culturally conditioned emotional revulsion is so strong that
he even avows he would rather see his own sons dope
addicts or murderers than see them become homosexuals.
One cannot help thinking what would be the suffering of
one of Epstein's sons if he should, God forbid, find himself
a homosexual. In an analogous way the homosexuals who
accept Curran's judgment must see themselves condemned
through no fault of their own to a life in which every
expression of human sexual love will only serve to deepen
the hold of an objectively sinful condition on themselves
and their loved ones, separating them further from God's
plan. In contradiction to the biblical message that it is by
love that one unites oneself to God, homosexuals must see

their deepest and most sincere human love as cutting themselves and their loved ones off from God.

Curran seems to accept the questionable theological position that every affliction is the result of sin and that the sins of parents are punished in their offspring. For he states at one point that homosexuality is "a result of sin," and appears to accept the unproven causal assumption that the homosexuality of the child is a result of sinful failures in parental relationships: "Those who accept an etiology of homosexuality in terms of relationships and environment can easily see the reality of sin in the poor relationships and environment which contribute to this condition in the individual."[10] Needless to say, this understanding of the source of homosexuality has been seriously discredited by many professional studies. As Dennis Altman notes:

> Many psychiatrists tend to locate the origins of homo-sexuality in "maladjusted" family life, yet such an ex-planation is not altogether convincing. Too many ho-mosexuals have strong and loving fathers, too many heterosexuals have dominating mothers, for any very obvious connection to be seen. It is probable that in Western societies most mothers overdominate their sons, and this fact is often disregarded by those con-cerned to discover the etiology of homosexuality.[11]

Psychologist Ray B. Arens also points out that some consid-eration must be given to the likelihood that the child's inner character at least partially determines parental reactions and attitudes toward him: "For instance, it is just as tenable to assume that the father of a pre-homosexual son becomes detached or hostile because he does not understand his son, is disappointed in him, or threatened by him, as it is to assume that the son becomes homosexual because of the father's reaction."[12]

What is particularly reprehensible about this dubious assumption of parental fault is the unproven burden of guilt it imposes on parents and the added impediment it places in the way of their children's being able to share their problem with their family. There are no necessary grounds for judging parents somehow responsible for their son's or daughter's homosexual condition; but there may well be grounds for judging them responsible for the disturbed or neurotic condition that all too frequently accompanies homosexuality. For the real moral problem that exists for the parents of a homosexual child is one of loving openness and acceptance. Whenever, in counseling, one has the good fortune to encounter psychologically healthy homosexuals, sure of their own dignity and their power to love and to be loved, one can be almost certain that their parents, whatever their disappointment over their children's condition, have responded to them with true acceptance and love. Parents of a homosexual have no reason to assume guilt for their child's condition; but parents of a psychologically healthy homosexual have good reason to believe that they have done their difficult task well.

Curran to all appearances never takes the human love which unites homosexual partners seriously. One is left with the impression that he reluctantly admits the possibility of homosexual liaisons in the same spirit as civil authorities who "reluctantly" license houses of prostitution, for his reason for condoning the existence of such liaisons is that they would be "better than homosexual promiscuity." In this respect it is interesting to note Curran's misinterpretation of my articles in the *Homiletic and Pastoral Review*.[13] At one point I conceded to those of my readers who could not understand or accept an ethic based in interpersonal love that they could, perhaps, accept homosexual relationships as morally valid from the traditional viewpoint of "the lesser of two evils." This was only one passing aspect of my argument for the possibility of "ethically responsible homosexual relationships," a passing attempt to conciliate those who could not free themselves from the need of a traditional peg on which to hang their moral judgments.[14] However, the entire thrust of my argument for morally acceptable homosexual relationships was that this form of sexual expression could be morally justified if it could be expressive of genuinely constructive human love.

It should come as no surprise, then, that all the qualities which morally justify a heterosexual human relationship—fidelity and permanence, for example—are systematically negated by Curran in the context of homosexual relationships. Instead of being able to form the intention of fidelity and permanence in their human love relationships to the best of their ability, homosexuals who accept Curran's judgment must see their relationships as being morally justifiable only as a temporary concession to their moral deformity. Thus they must continue to do everything in their power to correct their condition, or at least abstain from an active expression of it—and consequently bring any homosexual love relationship to an end. The most important question, however, still remains unanswered: What methodological and substantive considerations led Curran into all the ambiguities of his theory of compromise?

2
Scripture and Homosexuality

The Use of Scripture

There are two methodological questions in moral theology which are important for a discussion of the morality of homosexuality. The first of these has to do with the use and place of Scripture in moral theology, and the second with the use and place of the human sciences. Since a Christian ethics as such reflects on human reality within the context of Christian revelation, it is obvious that scriptural sources have a role to play: "Biblical ethics contributes data to Christian ethics, but it remains only one aspect, albeit a privileged aspect, of the total data of ethical theology," Father Curran notes. There are, however, two limitations to the use of biblical data. First, the Scriptures are "historically and culturally limited," so that one cannot merely transpose a text of Scripture to the contemporary circumstances of life. Second, no thesis would be acceptable which would develop its argument only in terms of individual texts taken out of their context.[1]

When Curran makes use of scriptural data concerning homosexuality, however, he does not seem to apply adequately the criteria he himself set down for a legitimate use of such data. Referring to those passages in the Old and New Testaments which have been traditionally translated as dealing with homosexuality, he acknowledges that "possibly erroneous interpretations seem to have overemphasized the heinousness of homosexual acts."[2] He accepts D. Sherwin Bailey's account of the Sodom story of Genesis 19:4–11, granting that the sin of the Sodomites "does not necessarily involve a sexual connotation but could be interpreted as a violation of hospitality."[3] This is a very important concession, since the centuries-old tradition in the Christian world of extreme condemnation of homosexuality always had its primary basis in the interpretation of this text of Genesis as indicating an extreme divine judgment of condemnation on homosexual behavior. He continues to accept, however, what he believes to be a general condemnation of homosexuality in the Old Testament. His primary evidence for this is the references to homosexuality in the Holiness Code (Lev. 18:22; 20:13), where it is referred to as a major crime punishable by death.

Indicating three direct references to homosexuality in the New Testament, all in the epistles of Saint Paul (1 Cor. 6:9–10; 1 Tim. 1:9–10; Rom. 1:26–27), Curran concludes: "Paul obviously regards homosexual acts as wrong and a perversion of human existence willed by God."[4] He acknowledges, however, Thielicke's contention that Paul's consideration of homosexuality appears "only in the context of a more central theological affirmation that disorder in the vertical dimension of man's relation with God is matched by disorder in the horizontal dimension."[5] Consequently, Paul never considers homosexuality in itself, but "only as illustrative of the central theological point that man's relationship with God affects all his other relationships."[6]

Curran concludes from this brief consideration of biblical data that it "indicates that the biblical authors in their cultural and historical circumstances deemed homosexual acts wrong and attached a generic gravity to such acts, but there appears to be no reason for attaching a special heinousness or gravity to these acts."[7] In all these considerations, however, he omits a central question. Can one merely accept what is referred to in English translations of the Bible as homosexuality as representing in the mind of the biblical authors what we refer to today by the same term?

We would do well to recall here the words of the Dogmatic Constitution on Divine Revelation of the Second Vatican Council dealing with the interpretation of sacred Scripture:

> Since God speaks in sacred Scripture through men in a human fashion, the interpreter of sacred Scripture, in order to see clearly what God wanted to communicate to us, should carefully investigate what meaning the sacred writers really intended, and what God wanted to manifest by means of their words. (No. 12)[8]

This cautious investigation of the intention of the human author is especially called for in dealing with biblical passages which traditionally have been accepted as dealing with homosexual activity.

The Need for a Definition of Homosexuality

Unfortunately, Curran never attempts to define exactly what he means by the term homosexual. As a result he feels free to assume that what is usually translated in the biblical texts by the same term as that used today actually refers to the same condition. It can, however, be argued (1) that what is referred to, especially in the New Testament, under the rubric of homosexuality is not the same reality at all or (2) that the biblical authors do not manifest the same understanding of that reality as we have today. Further, it can be seriously questioned whether what is understood today as the true homosexual and his or her activity is ever the object of explicit moral condemnation in Scripture.

The prefix *homo-* in the word homosexual is derived from the Greek root meaning "same," and not from the Latin word for "man." Consequently, it designates anyone who is sexually attracted to someone of the same sex and includes both male and female homosexuals, or lesbians. Most human beings are capable of either homosexual or heterosexual activity, independent of the question of their own psychological sexual orientation. Many homosexuals marry and have children, frequently in an effort to conceal their sexual orientation. On the other hand, there is no necessary connection between overt homosexual behavior and the permanent psychological condition of homosexuality. Many people have had homosexual experiences who do not have a predominantly homosexual orientation but are definitely heterosexually inclined. Consequently, it is important for the moralist to keep the distinction between homosexual activity and the homosexual condition clearly in mind. For there is an important difference in the moral judgment to be passed on a heterosexual indulging in homosexual activity and a true homosexual indulging in the same behavior as an expression of his or her love.

Kinsey limited himself exclusively to objective behavior in the scientific study he made of sexual mores in the United States, leaving aside the subjective question of the sexual orientation of his respondents. According to Kinsey, as much as thirty-seven percent of the male population had some overt homosexual experience.[9] In the majority of cases, however, these experiences seemed to involve little more than transitory experimentation which did not inhibit a later satisfactory heterosexual adjustment. There are many other forms of contingent homosexual practice which can be called situational and which do not indicate a true homosexual psychological condition. When, for example, men are isolated together for long periods of time and separated from the companionship of women—as in prisons or at sea—many will adopt homosexual behavior; but most of them normally discard their homosexual behavior and resume a heterosexual orientation once withdrawn from their segregated situation. Still other forms of conditional homosexual behavior, which do not necessarily indicate a homosexual condition, can be called variational, e.g., heterosexuals who occasionally take part in homosexual activity out of curiosity or as an easy means of sexual indulgence. Still one other form of conditional homosexual behavior should be mentioned. This category involves people who, although they are fundamentally heterosexually inclined, adopt homosexual behavior consequent upon some traumatic event or psychic disorder. If they are cured of their trauma or disorder, they will revert to their original heterosexual inclination.

Although all of the above groups have had some homosexual experience, none of them are what could be called "true" homosexuals. Today we use the word homosexual primarily to refer to the psychic condition of the individual, and not just to occasional behavior. Bailey defines homosexuality as "a condition characterized by an emotional and physico-sexual propensity toward others of the same sex."[10] D. W. Cory defines the homosexual as "any person who feels a most urgent sexual desire which in the main is directed toward gratification with the same sex."[11] The Dutch Catechism uses the term to refer to those "whose eroticism cannot be directed to the other sex, but apparently only to the same sex to which they themselves belong."[12] As John Cavanaugh remarks, "It is important to accept the concept that homosexuality is a way of thinking and feeling, not merely a way of acting. The performance of homosexual acts is, therefore, not in itself evidence of homosexuality."[13] Christopher Isherwood indicates the subjective norm for knowing oneself to be a homosexual when he writes: "You first *know* you are a homosexual when you fall in love with another man."[14]

As Bailey observes, strictly speaking neither the Bible nor Christian tradition knew anything of homosexuality as such; both were concerned solely with the commission of homosexual acts.[15] Homosexuality is not, as commonly supposed, a kind of conduct, but a psychological condition. It is important to understand that the genuine homosexual condition—or inversion, as it is often termed—is something for which the subject can in no way be held responsible. In itself it is morally neutral. Like the condition of heterosexuality, however, it tends to find expression in specific sexual acts; and such acts are subject to moral judgment. We must distinguish, then, between the invert and the pervert. The pervert is not a genuine homosexual; rather, he is a heterosexual who engages in homosexual practices, or a homosexual who engages in heterosexual practices. This distinction between the condition of inversion and the behavior of perversion is indispensable for a correct interpretation of biblical and traditional sources.

The real moral problem of homosexuality has to do with judging the moral value of sexual activity between genuine homosexuals who seek to express their love for one another in a sexual gesture. Scripture can be understood as clearly and explicitly condemning true homosexual activity only if it can be interpreted as condemning the activity of a true invert. To such situations, however, it can hardly be said that the Bible addresses itself, since the condition of inversion with all its special problems was quite unknown at the time. On the contrary, there is ample evidence that in most instances where Scripture deals with homosexuality the author probably had in mind what today we would call perversion, namely, the indulgence in homosexual activity on the part of those who were by nature heterosexually inclined.

The Sodom and Gomorrah Story in Genesis

Perhaps the single most important factor in the Western Christian tradition condemning homosexual practices is the interpretation given to the Sodom and Gomorrah story in Genesis 19:4–11.[16] The Church taught, and people universally believed on what they held to be excellent authority, that homosexual practices had brought a terrible divine vengeance upon the cities of Sodom and Gomorrah, and that the repetition of such "offenses against nature" had from time to time provoked similar visitations of divine wrath in the form of earthquakes, floods, famines, outbreaks of pestilence, etc. It was taken for granted, therefore, that by means of both Church discipline and the restraints and penalties of civil law steps should be taken to ward off the wrath of God from the community. It was also taken for granted that the sin for which the cities of the plain were destroyed was that of the habitual indulgence of perverse homosexual practices among men. Consequently, the question must be posed: To what extent is this tradition truly founded in Scripture? What was the meaning of the encounter of Lot and his angelic visitors with the angry inhabitants of Sodom as recorded by the Yahwist author of Genesis 19? Finally, what grounds, if any, are there for the persistent belief that the inhabitants of the city were addicted to male homosexual practices and were punished accordingly?

As D. S. Bailey points out, the attribution of homosexual practices is based usually on the demand the Sodomites are recorded to have made of Lot: "Bring them [Lot's visitors] out unto us, that we may know them." The Hebrew word "to know" (yādhā) can mean "engage in coitus." However,

Bailey argues this is not necessarily the meaning of the word in this passage. The Hebrew-English Lexicon of the Old Testament notes that of the 943 uses of *yādhả*, it is used only 10 times without qualification, apart from this text in Genesis and its derivative in Judges 19:22, to denote sexual coitus. And, again with the possible exception of this text, it always refers to heterosexual coitus. The word normally used in the Old Testament for both homosexual coitus and bestiality is *shākhabh*. G. A. Barton concludes from this evidence that "there is no actual necessity to interpret 'know' in Gen. xix, 5 as equivalent with 'to have coitus with.' It may mean no more than 'get acquainted with.' "[17]

Bailey argues further that the passage can be interpreted as implying that Lot, who was a *gēr* or resident alien in Sodom, may have exceeded his rights by receiving and entertaining two foreigners whose intentions might have been hostile and whose credentials, it seems, had not been examined. This explanation provides a natural and sufficient reason for the demand: "Where are the men who came to thee this night? Bring them out unto us, that we may know them."

What, then, Bailey asks, was the nature of the sinfulness of Sodom and Gomorrah? We are told in the passage itself in Genesis that these cities were wicked and grievously sinful, but the writer does not specify the nature of this iniquity more exactly. However, Bailey argues, only on a priori grounds can it be assumed that it was an iniquity solely or even predominantly sexual in character. There is no evidence elsewhere in the passage or in the Old Testament to show that homosexual behavior was particularly prevalent in these cities. Lot's offer to surrender his daughters in place of the strangers is sometimes interpreted as an offer of heterosexual in lieu of homosexual satisfaction, in order to divert the lust of the Sodomites into less inordinate channels. However, Bailey claims, this episode can be reasonably explained as simply the most tempting bribe Lot could offer at the spur of the moment to appease a hostile crowd.

Bailey believes that for an understanding of the development of the Sodom and Gomorrah story it is important to place it in the context of the legends of a similar character in the folklore of the surrounding cultures. Many of these legends tell of a stranger (sometimes a divine being in disguise) who visits a prosperous city and is refused hospitality. He eventually finds a lodging, often with poor outcasts. Consequently, he helps his hosts escape before the city and its inhabitants are destroyed. The most famous of these legends is Ovid's account of Philemon and Baucis.[18] These legends may account for the particular form the Sodom story itself assumed during its course of oral transmission prior to being written down. In the legend, as in the same Yahwist author's Tower of Babel narrative in Genesis 11:9, the conduct which brings judgment upon the offending community and leads to its destruction is never sexual, but always wickedness in general, and in particular pride and inhospitality.

There are several other aspects to the narrative, besides those Bailey mentions, which tend to indicate that in the mind of the Yahwist author of the narrative the sin of Sodom and Gomorrah was primarily one of inhospitality to strangers. For example, when the angelic visitors come as strangers to Abraham's tent, the quality of Abraham as a good man is dramatically established by an emphasis on his hospitable reception of the strangers.

> Raising his eyes he saw three men standing near him.
> On seeing them, he ran from the door of his tent to
> meet them, and bowing to the ground said; "Oh sirs, if
> perchance I find favor with you, please do not pass by
> without stopping with your servant. Let a little water

be brought to wash your feet, and stretch yourselves
out under the tree, while I fetch a bit of food that you
may refresh yourselves. Afterwards you may proceed
on your way, since you will then have paid your servant a visit." (Gen. 18:1–5)[19]

Similarly the quality of Lot as a good man worthy of God's
favor is established in contrast to the other inhabitants of
Sodom by his hospitality to the same strangers in terms
strongly reminiscent of the story of the disciples of Emmaus
in the New Testament:

The two angels arrived at Sodom in the evening while
Lot was sitting at the gate of Sodom. When Lot saw
them, he rose to greet them, bowing his face to the
ground, and saying: "If you please, sirs, come over to
your servant's house to pass the night and wash your
feet; in the morning you may rise early, and go on your
way." But they said: "No, we will pass the night in the
open." He pressed them so strongly, however, that
they went over to his house, where he prepared a feast
for them, and baked unleavened bread for them to eat.
(Gen. 19:1–3)

A confirmation of the interpretation of the primary sin of
Sodom and Gomorrah as inhospitality occurs in the New
Testament where Christ is recorded as discussing the
problem of the inhospitable reception of his disciples:

But whenever you come to a town and they do not
welcome you, go out into the open streets and say:
"The very dust of your town that sticks to our feet we
wipe off in protest. But understand this: The Kingdom
of God is at hand!" I tell you, on that day Sodom will
fare better than that town! (Lk. 10:10–13)

Throughout the Old Testament Sodom is referred to as a symbol of utter destruction occasioned by sins of such magnitude as to merit exemplary punishment.[20] However, nowhere in the Old Testament is that sin identified explicitly with homosexual behavior. In Ezekiel 16:49–50, for example, we read: "Behold, this was the sin of your sister Sodom: she and her daughter lived in pride, plenty, and thoughtless ease; they supported not the poor and needy; they grew haughty, and committed abomination before me; so I swept them away, as you have seen." Isaiah stresses lack of justice, Jeremiah cites moral and ethical laxity. The Deuterocanonical books usually identify the sin as one of pride and inhospitality. Wisdom (19:13–14), for example, clearly identifies the sin as one of inhospitality: "whereas the men of Sodom received not the strangers when they came among them; the Egyptians made slaves of the guests who were their benefactors." Ecclesiasticus (16:8) in turn identifies the sin as pride: "He did not spare the people among whom Lot was living, whom he detested for their pride." Only the late New Testament books, 2 Peter and Jude, find the sin of Sodom connected in any way with sexual practices; but these books, as we shall discuss later, seem to understand the sin as a "transgression of orders" between human and angelic beings.

A further confirmation that in biblical times the sin of Sodom was not connected with homosexual practices as such is to be found in the fact that none of the biblical passages, either in the Old or New Testament, traditionally understood as condemning these practices makes any mention of the Sodom story. Yet such a reference would have been obvious if the sin of Sodom was understood as involving these practices.

It would seem fairly certain, then, that the sin of Sodom was understood in biblical times as primarily one of inhospitality. However, Bailey may perhaps have overstated his case in maintaining that there is no reference at all to sexual mistreatment of the strangers as one aspect of the crime of inhospitality. There is a hint of this in the fact that the same Hebrew word *yādhá* is used again by Lot in verse 7 when he offers his daughters to the inhabitants, and here it clearly and unambiguously implies sexual knowledge:

> Please my friends, be not so depraved. I have two
> daughters who have never had intercourse [*yādhá*]
> with a man, let me bring them out to you that you may
> do with them what you will; only do nothing to these
> men, inasmuch as they have come under the shelter of
> my roof. (Gen. 19:7–8)

It remains possible, however, that the Yahwist author was deliberately playing on the ambiguity of the term, using it in two different meanings.

Further, Bailey's interpretation makes it difficult to understand how the behavior of the inhabitants of Sodom confirmed the angels' opinion that they were wicked enough to deserve divine punishment, if they only wished to examine their credentials. In the derivative account of the crime of Gibeah in the Book of Judges (19:1–21:25), the identical request is made of the old man, who takes in the stranger for the night, by the inhabitants of Gibeah. In this instance, however, the stranger releases his female consort to the crowd, and they so misuse her sexually that the stranger finds her dead on the threshold in the morning. At a consequent gathering of the tribes of Israel, the stranger makes clear what the crime of Gibeah was:

> To Gibeah, which belongs to the Benjamin, I came
> with my consort to spend the night; but the citizens of
> Gibeah rose against me, and at night surrounded the
> house against me. Me they intended to kill, and my
> consort they ravished, so that she died. (Judg. 20:4–6)

In the book of Judges' derivative, then, the crime of inhospitality included the design to murder the stranger. The obvious stress, once again, is not so much on the implied sexual contact with the stranger as on the right of the stranger to a hospitable reception. John McKenzie's comment on the crime of Gibeah is equally applicable to the Sodom story:

> They [the authors] here betray two convictions . . . the absolute sacredness of the guest and the absolute dignity of the male sex. The duty of the host to protect the guest we can understand, but not to the point where the honor and the life of the women of the family are regarded as expendable.[21]

As we shall note later, the idea of "the absolute dignity of the male sex" was one of the factors underlying the Jewish hostility to male homosexual practices.

Peter Ellis, in his book *The Yahwist: The Bible's First Theologian,* offers an interesting and suggestive thesis to explain the possible presence of the sexual element in the Sodom narrative. He points out that one of the Yahwist author's principal themes was an attack against Canaanite nature worship directed to the fertility gods. Speaking of the episode in Genesis concerning the "sons of God" lusting after the daughters of men, he writes:

> The Yahwist's audience would certainly recognize in the story an allusion to the ludicrous belief of the Canaanite religion that by means of sacred prostitution— sexual intercourse with male and female prostitutes at the Canaanite shrines—it was possible to enter into special relationship with the god or goddess represented by the sacred prostitute.[22]

In the fertility-cult ritual, sacred prostitution climaxed the rite which hailed the return of the rains and fertility. "In the punishment which follows the fornication of the sons of God with the daughters of men the rains came with a vengeance. The floods cover the earth, and everything upon its fertile surface is swept away by cleansing waters."[23]

Ellis suggests that the same polemic against the fertility rites is to be found in the Sodom narrative. "For their crimes, which the author indicates were the unnatural sexual vices the Canaanites had made part of their fertility rites, the five plain cities are wiped off the map."[24] The same connection between homosexual practices and idolatry which, as we shall see, is present in all the biblical passages is also present here. Again, the punishment is a "rain"; this time a rain of fire and brimstone, and the result is a barren earth on which nothing will ever grow. Even in this interpretation, the primary crime of Sodom is idolatry, and not homosexual practices as such but these practices as an expression of sacred prostitution.

We shall deal later, under the heading of tradition, with the gradual historical development which transformed the understanding of the sin of Sodom in Western Christian tradition from a sin primarily of inhospitality to the stranger to one of homosexual practices. At this point we can conclude, however, that the most important biblical basis for the traditional condemnation of homosexual practices as clearly against the express will of God proves on examination the most vulnerable. It has been accepted practically without question that God himself declared his judgment upon homosexual practices once and for all time by the destruction of the cities of the plain. But the Sodom and Gomorrah narrative possibly had nothing whatever to do with such practices. Even if one continues to hold that there is a suggestion of the presence of this sexual element, it does not constitute the essence of the sin of Sodom and Gomorrah. Rather, the sin remains primarily one of inhospitality. And even if Ellis is correct, the homosexual practices are condemned not in themselves but as part of the idolatrous fertility cult of the Canaanites.

If this interpretation of the true sin of Sodom is correct, then we are dealing here with one of the supremely ironic paradoxes of history. For thousands of years in the Christian West homosexuals have been the victim of inhospitable treatment. Condemned by the Church, they have been the victim of persecution, torture, and even death. In the name of a mistaken understanding of the crime of Sodom and Gomorrah, the true crime of Sodom and Gomorrah has been and continues to be repeated every day. Before advancing to an examination of the Sodom story in tradition, let us first examine the other passages in the Old and New Testaments understood as condemning homosexual practices.

Problems of Translation

Two Greek words in 1 Cor. 6:9 are usually translated as having to do with homosexuality; they are *malakoi* and *arsenokoitai*. The second term occurs again in 1 Tim. 1:10. There is a venerable tradition in English translations of the Bible to assume that these terms apply to homosexual activity. The King James version translates them as "neither the effeminate nor the abusers of themselves with mankind" and the Rheims-Douai version similarly speaks of the "effeminate"and "liers with mankind." The first edition of the Revised Standard version translates both terms with the one word "homosexuals." The only major variation of this tradition is to be found in the Jerusalem Bible, which uses the terms "catamites and sodomites," and the Smith-Good-speed (Chicago) Bible, which renders them as "sensual" and those "given to unnatural vices." It is interesting to note that the Spanish version of the Jerusalem Bible uses "los homosexuales," whereas the French version speaks of "dépravés" and "gens de moeurs infames." As John Boswell notes: "Cultural differences appear to exercise considerable influence over the translation of Biblical passages dealing with sexual morality."[25] Bailey particularly takes to task the translators of the Revised Standard version for their use of the single term "homosexuals":

> But the translation approved by those responsible for the American Revised Standard version is unfortunately both inaccurate and objectionable . . . it is most regrettable that the reviewers should have shown themselves unaware or unappreciative of the clear distinction which must be made between the homosexual *condition* (which is morally neutral) and homosexual *practices*. Use of the word "homosexuals" inevitably suggests the genuine invert, even though he be a man of irreproachable morals, is automatically branded as unrighteous and excluded from the kingdom of God, just as if he were the most depraved of sexual perverts.[26]

The variation in translations points to the fact that there is very little understanding of the precise meaning of Paul's terms. What is needed is a contextual analysis and an examination of the same terms in other sources. It is truly surprising that despite the fact that the tradition of moral condemnation of homosexuality springs in large part from these biblical passages, little serious scholarly work has been produced concerning their exact meaning. Translations appear at times to be based on preconceptions rather than serious scholarship.

The immediate context itself gives little or no clue as to the precise meaning Paul intended by these words. In the Corinthian passage Paul lists the types of sinners who are to be excluded from the kingdom of God; and in the Timothy passage, those who have not received the law of God.

S. Wibbing argues that Paul derived these lists from the popular Stoic list of excesses contrary to reason.[27] Both lists have been recognized by scholars as remarkably confusing, and the context is quite loose. Consequently we must turn to the use of the same terms in other sources to discover their meaning. The word *malakos* literally means soft (e.g., Luke 7:25; Mt. 11:8). In a moral context it is normally employed to signify loose, morally weak, or lacking in self-control. There is no justification for applying *malakos* specifically to homosexuality. In patristic Greek *malakia* usually referred to generally dissolute behavior and occasionally referred to specific sexual activity such as masturbation, but never to homosexuality as such. It could conceivably include that, but its normal use referred to any form of immorality. I need not stress the point here that the concept of "effeminacy" has no necessary connection with homosexuality.[28]

Before considering the second word, *arsenokoitai*, it is important to recall to mind that there was no word in classical, biblical, or patristic Greek with the same meaning as the English word homosexual. In those pre-Freudian days neither the Greeks nor the Romans recognized homosexuality as a psychological phenomenon or condition apart from general sexual behavior. There appears to be no consciousness of a dichotomy such as the modern homosexual versus heterosexual. There were names, however, for persons who practiced homosexual activity. They included, for example, *paiderastēs, pallakos, kinaidos, arrenomanēs,* and *paidophthoros*. If it were Paul's intention to indicate general homosexual activity as such, it is probable that he would have selected one of these terms.

The word *arsenokoitai*, then, probably does not refer to general homosexual behavior. However, what Paul did mean by it is difficult to ascertain. The use of the noun in the plural does not occur in Greek literature before the Pauline text. Apart from a second-century use of the same word in the *Apology* of Aristides, where from the context it seems to mean "an obsessive corruptor of boys,"[29] the most important usage for the purpose of clearer definition occurs in the sixth-century *Penitentiale* of Joannes Jejunator, Patriarch of Constantinople in 586 under Mauritius.[30] Here it designates a specific sex act, most likely anal intercourse. Nor does this refer exclusively to homosexuality, since in a later passage use is made of the same term to refer to a sex act between men and women.[31]

Some indication of what Paul might have meant by the term can be derived from his use of *koitai* in the plural. For this usage appears to refer to excess in sexual behavior (cf. Rom. 13:13). It is possible that the author attached to the compound a meaning like "male prostitution." This interpretation is borne out by the Vulgate rendering *masculi concubitores*, that is, male concubines. As we shall see, this interpretation will be strengthened by the more general context of the Old Testament where male prostitution was usually associated with the same context of idolatry.

The Interpretation of Romans 1:26

The strongest New Testament argument against homosexual activity as intrinsically immoral has been derived traditionally from Romans 1:26, where this activity is indicated as *para physin*. The normal English translation for this phrase has been "against nature." As John Boswell notes: "The modern reader is apt to read into that phrase a wealth of associations derived from later philosophical developments, scholastic theology, Freudian psychology, social taboos, as well as personal misgivings."[32] Once again it is difficult to ascertain what this phrase meant for Paul. The same phrase in Romans 4:18 is used to express the idea that God himself is acting *para physin* in grafting a wild olive branch (the Gentiles) onto a cultivated tree (the inheritance of the Jews). This usage makes it clear that the phrase itself does not necessarily imply a moral judgment on the action as wrong.

From an examination of the seven uses of the word *physis* in the epistles of Paul, one can begin to understand what Paul meant by the word. Although it is most likely that Paul accepted the phrase from the popular Stoic philosophy of the day, he does not necessarily indicate an intrinsic nature or essence in the philosophical sense, such as would serve the basis of a natural-law judgment. Rather, it is always linked to religious and cultural heritage. The Jews are Jews "by nature" (Gal. 2:15); and the Gentiles are uncircumcised "by nature" (Rom. 2:27). Although we are all "by nature" children of wrath (Eph. 2:3), the Gentiles can do "by nature"—i.e., by custom without hearing the word— the things of the law (Rom. 2:14). With the exception of Gal. 4:8, where reference is made to men who "by nature" are not gods, the character referred to by *physis* does not necessarily represent something that is innate, but could be a matter of training and social conditioning. This is evident, for example, in 1 Cor. 11:14: "Does not nature teach you that, if a man has long hair, it is a shame unto him?"

When he uses the word nature Paul does not make a sharp distinction between natural law and social custom. For example, in the phrase *tēn physikēn kresin* (Rom. 1:26) Paul does not make the distinction between nature and custom which was common among educated Greeks of the time (e.g., *Ignatius to the Trallians* 1.1: "either against custom [*kresin*] or nature [*physin*]"). Rather, he tends to fuse together the concepts of custom and essential character. There seems to be a parallel in Paul's mind between what is *para physin* and the Old Testament concept of *toevah*, i.e., what is not proper according to Jewish law and custom.

Consequently, two interpretations can be justified concerning what Paul meant by the phrase. It could refer to the

individual pagan, who goes beyond his own sexual appetites in order to indulge in new sexual pleasures. A strong
argument for this interpretation is the explicit reference to
the pagans having "abandoned" the "natural uses" of their
sexuality for that which is "beyond nature." The use here of
the aorist participle (*aphentes*) considerably strengthens
the image of a conscious choice of a type of activity contrary
to their normal inclinations. Paul apparently refers only to
homosexual acts indulged in by those he considered to be
otherwise heterosexually inclined; acts which represent a
voluntary choice to act contrary to their ordinary sexual
appetite. William G. Thompson, S.J., is inclined to agree
with this interpretation:

> Concerning the Pauline material, you have come to the
> same conclusions I have concerning the meaning of
> "homosexual." Let me quote Fr. Fitzmyer's comments
> on Romans 1:26: "The contrast between 'females' and
> 'males' (1:27) makes it clear that the sexual perversion
> of which Paul speaks is homosexuality (specifically
> Lesbianism). The depravity of the perversion is the
> merited consequence of pagan impiety; having
> exchanged their true God for a false one (1:25), pagans
> inevitably exchanged their true natural functions for
> perverted ones . . . (Jerome Biblical Commentary, Arti-
> cle 53, Number 26)." It seems clear that the situation is
> one of perversion rather than inversion, as you indi-
> cate. Hence the passage does not touch the contempo-
> rary issue of homosexuality understood as inversion.
> Paul simply does not speak to that question.

The second possibility is that *physis* refers to the "nature"
of the chosen people who were forbidden by Levitical law
to have homosexual relations. Paul can be understood as
arguing that the recognition of the true God necessarily
involves acceptance of the Levitical law. Both interpreta-

tions are probably valid. Paul seems to be implying that the Gentiles, having known the truth of God and rejecting it, as a result reject their true nature as regards their sexual appetites, going beyond what was natural to them (heterosexual activity) and what was approved for the Jews.

Consequently, the Pauline epistles do not explicitly treat of the problem of homosexual activity between persons who share the homosexual condition, and as such cannot be read as explicitly condemning such behavior. Neither the *malakoi* nor the *arsenokoitai* were necessarily homosexuals; the former were simply debauched individuals and the latter were probably male prostitutes or those given to anal intercourse, which is not necessarily nor exclusively a homosexual activity. The persons referred to in Romans 1:26 are probably not homosexuals—i.e., those who are psychologically inclined toward their own sex—since they are portrayed as "abandoning their natural customs." Moreover, the ambiguity of Paul's use of the word *physis* as including what is customary precludes an interpretation of the passage as condemning homosexual activity as intrinsically evil independent of the actors' condition and their social laws and customs.

The Old Testament Context

Because of his Jewish background Paul obviously found the rampant homosexuality he observed in Greece very shocking. His main point was always that the prevalence of homosexual activity was a sign of alienation from God. He obviously had in mind the Old Testament prohibition of homosexual activity. Consequently, we must note the context of the texts within the Old Testament in which the question of homosexual activity is treated. Homosexual activity was definitely connected in Jewish consciousness with idolatry. An example of this is to be found in Deuteronomy 23:17:

> None of the Israelite women shall become a temple-prostitute, nor shall any of the Israelite men become a temple-prostitute. You shall never bring the gains of a harlot or the earnings of a male prostitute as a votive offering to the temple of the Lord your God; for both are abominable to the Lord your God.

It was a practice among some of Israel's neighbors to use both sexes as part of the fertility rites in temple services. Since the gods were understood as sexual, they were to be worshiped in overt sexual acts. Whenever homosexual activity is mentioned in the Old Testament, the author usually has in mind the use male worshipers made of male prostitutes provided by the temple authorities.

Paul was well aware of this context from the Old Testament. In reading Paul, it is important to keep in mind what Thielicke refers to as Paul's "central concern" in the text dealing with homosexual activity, especially Romans 1:26. Paul obviously believed that homosexual activity, as far as he understood it, was the result of idolatry. As Wood points out, one must remember the sequence of events as Paul portrays them in Romans.[33] A person is not idolatrous because he or she is a homosexual; that person is, however, involved in homosexual activities because he or she is idolatrous. God punished idolaters by delivering them over to their selfishness and passions. It would appear, then, that Paul treats of homosexual activities only within the context of idol worship. The Holiness Code (Lev. 18:22, 20:13) originally established the connection between idolatry and homosexual activity. The Code specifically warns the Israelites against accepting the idolatrous practices of the Canaanites. One of the provisions of the Code is that homosexual activity is punishable by death.

Several other cultural and historical circumstances ought also to be considered. One must keep in mind the pro-fertility bent of the Old Testament authors that was due to underpopulation, with the result that any willful destruc-tion of viable human seed was regarded as a serious crime. Another factor influencing the Old Testament attitude on homosexual activity was the strong Hebrew stress on pre-serving the family name through progeny. In fact, partici-pation in God's covenant with the chosen people depended on having children. One of the worst curses which could befall a Jewish male was sterility.

Still another contextual factor has to do with the common use in biblical times of the act of sodomy as an expression of domination, contempt, and scorn. According to J. Edgar Brun, the ultimate "why" of the wrongness of homosexual activity in Israelite eyes can best be discerned in the account of Noah and his sons after the flood (Gen. 9:18–27). The second part of the story has obviously been expurgated and revised. The Hebrew makes it quite clear that Ham did not merely look at his father but actually did something to him. Yet whereas Ham is the wrongdoer, Canaan, his son, is the person cursed. Brun believes the story was undoubt-edly an anti-Egyptian polemic and searches to reconstruct it with an episode in the Egyptian epic entitled *The Contend-ing of Horus and Seth* (XI:3–4).

Horus was the posthumous son and heir of the god Osiris, the primordial king and giver of life. He was invited by his uncle, Seth, to spend a day. Seth's real motive was not to show him hospitality but to disqualify him from inheriting his father's royal power. To this end, while Horus slept Seth committed an act of sodomy upon him. Since sodomy was inflicted as a punishment on a defeated enemy and was a symbol of domination, Seth could then claim that he had conquered Horus and demand the kingship in his place. Brun claims that the original biblical story followed the same line: "By committing sodomy upon his father, who was the ancestor of all men after the flood . . . Ham (Egypt) could also claim the right to dominate all mankind."[34] The revision, which omits any explicit reference to a sexual act and makes Canaan the recipient of Noah's curse, was prompted by the fact that the Canaanites had become the immediate threat to Israel's political and religious survival.

Calling attention then to the common practice, especially of the Egyptians, of inflicting sodomy as a punishment upon a defeated male enemy as a symbol of domination, Brun suggests that the principal reason the Israelites regarded homosexual practices as an abomination was that

> they too viewed sodomy as an expression of scorn; and in a society where the dignity of the male was a primary consideration, voluntary acts of a homosexual nature could not be tolerated. Both parties would then be undermining the very foundations of a patriarchal society; the one because he uses another as a woman; the other because he allows himself to be used as a woman. The dignity of the male is dishonored by both.[35]

We have already seen McKenzie's comment that one of the aims of the narrator of the crime of Gibeah was to establish the absolute dignity of the male. It is interesting to note that the Holiness Code only condemns male homosexuality; no mention is made of female homosexual practices, but there is a condemnation under penalty of death of any woman who has sexual relations with an animal.

As Herman van de Spijker notes in his summary of biblical teaching concerning homosexual activities, both in the Old and the New Testaments, wherever the Bible clearly seems to refer to homosexual activity, we must recognize a judgment of condemnation. However, every text dealing with homosexual activity also refers to aggravating circumstances such as idolatry, sacred prostitution, promiscuity, violent rape, seduction of children, and violation of guests' rights. As a result one can never be sure to what extent the condemnation is of homosexual activities as such or only of homosexual activities under these circumstances: "Nowhere is there a specific text which explicitly rejects all homosexual activities as such independent of the circumstances." Van de Spijker is nevertheless of the opinion that such an objective universal condemnation can be deduced from these texts taken in conjunction with the biblical image of humankind in the creation account of Genesis; he concludes that "all homosexual relationships, even when they are true expressions of an I-thou relationship, are *objectively* contrary to nature as the order of creation.[36]

The Creation Account in Genesis

There are two accounts in Genesis of the creation of human sexuality. The first account, a version dated around 550–500 B.C., is from the Priestly tradition: "So God created man in his own image, in the image of God he created him, male and female he created them." This account clearly indicates that the divine purpose in creating sexual differentiation was procreation. Consequently, the first covenant between God and humanity was a procreative covenant. "And God blessed them and said to them: 'Be fruitful and multiply, and fill the earth and subdue it. . . . '"

However, according to scholars the second account, attributed to the Yahwist author, is much more ancient, dated 950 B.C. In this account God's purpose in creating sexual differentiation is not associated with procreation; rather, the purpose was companionship and a cure for loneliness: "Then the Lord God said, 'It is not good that the man

should be alone; I will make him a helper fit for him.' "
Thus mutual love and fulfillment is equally a biblical norm
for human sexuality. Many moralists seem to ignore the
significance of the Yahwists' account of creation and assume
that procreation is the only biblical norm.

There is, then, another and perhaps more important
reason apart from individual texts why some moralists
believe that all homosexual activity is condemned in Scripture as contrary to the will of God for man. This reason has
to do with the interpretation they give to the creation
account in Genesis. As Neale Secor argues, many Christian
ethicists read a condemnation of all homosexual activity
into the texts dealing specifically with that question because they are reading these particular texts with a basic
assumption. The assumption is that the homosexual condition is the result of humanity's fall and is a deviation from
the God-willed state of heterosexuality as expressed in the
creation. Under this assumption sexual differentiation is not
only normative for human relations; it assumes a metaphys-
ical significance in the very constitution of what is essentially human. "To be human becomes by hypothesis to be
purely male or female. Only in monogamous marriage
desirous of reproduction is this essential duality held in
balance."[37] In the Priestly tradition of the Old Testament,
the human male apart from the human female was not
considered a full human being. As Rabbi El'azar put it:
"Any Jew who has no wife is no man."[38]

Curran appears to be in agreement with this position. As
he sees it, human sexuality derives its meaning exclusively
"in terms of a relationship of male and female in a procreative union of love."[39] To defend this position he makes a
general appeal to scriptural data. "The scriptural data
undoubtedly points in this direction, even to the possible
extent that the likeness to God is precisely in terms of the
sexuality by which men and women are able to enter into a

covenant of love with one another." In the opinion of Karl
Barth, "man and woman—in the relationship conditioned
by this irreversible order—are the human creatures of God
and as such the image of God and likeness of the covenant
of grace."[40] Since man's likeness to God is to be found in
his power to love, some moralists find it necessary to read
into that love relationship the specific reality of heterosexual love, almost to the exclusion of all other forms of human
community and human love. They tend to identify the
biblical concept of person with heterosexual orientation
and find in that orientation the divine image in humanity.

In contrast with this understanding of the scriptural data
is T. C. DeKruijf's study, *The Bible on Sexuality*. DeKruijf
concludes his survey of Old Testament texts concerning
sexual morality by pointing out that the primary message of
the Old Testament concerning sexual morality was that
love, including sexual love, requires respect for the other
person; and the sin which one can commit in sexual
conduct with another consists in dishonoring the person of
a fellow human being. "If one does not acknowledge the
only true personal God, it follows unavoidably that one will
also not acknowledge one's fellow man as a person who has
a value of his own."[41] As we have seen, J. Edgar Brun found
an identical reason for the condemnation of homosexual
activities, since in the cultural and historical context of the
Old Testament such activities could only be envisaged as
expressions of hatred and scorn. The essential evil of
homosexual activities appeared to be the dishonoring of a
fellow human being.

DeKruijf points out, however, a very important difference
between the treatment of sexuality in the Old and the New
Testament. Marriage no longer plays the same role in the
New Testament that it did in the Old. In the Old Testament
"contact with God was connected with their being the
people of God, because in this chosen people God dealt

with man. Therefore it was important for every man and woman in Israel to receive this life and pass it on in marriage."[42] To understand the difference of viewpoint in the New Testament it is important to remember that the new people of God are no longer bound by blood relationship; membership in the new people of God is no longer a question of human descent. Consequently, marriage no longer occupies the central place it had in Israel. "In the New Covenant it is given to anyone to be fertile in the new people of God through a love which surpasses even marital love in value and therefore in fertility."[43] This new understanding of love lies at the origin of other vocational choices besides marriage, such as a life of sexual abstinence, and other forms of human community, such as the celibate community. One can no longer identify the love between humans that makes them the likeness of God univocally with the heterosexual relationship in marriage.

Another important difference between the Old and New Testaments concerning human sexuality has to do with the belief in personal immortality. For the most part in the Old Testament there was little stress on personal immortality; rather, stress was placed on the survival of the "people" and one's own survival in and through one's children. However, the New Testament emphasis on resurrection carried with it the belief in personal immortality and, consequently, freed the individual from the necessity of marrying and bearing children in order to achieve a form of survival beyond the grave. This change of emphasis is of particular interest vis-à-vis the homosexual, since, as many psychologists point out, one of the most profound roots of homophobia is the connection, unconscious for the most part, between homosexuality, barrenness, and death.

Nowhere is this new attitude concerning human sexuality more evident than in the account of the baptism of the Ethiopian eunuch in the Acts of the Apostles (8:26–39). The

Lucan author had as his purpose to depict the work of the Holy Spirit in the formation of the first Christian community and how that community differed from its predecessor. He stresses that people who were considered outcasts by Israel for various reasons were to be included in the new community. The first group are the Samaritans. The second group, symbolized by the eunuch, are those who for sexual reasons were excluded from the Old Testament community. "No one who has had his testicles crushed or his penis cut off shall marry into the Lord's community" (Deut. 23:1). However, in Isaiah 56:2–8 there is an explicit prophecy that with the coming of the Messiah and the establishment of the new covenant the eunuch, who was formerly excluded from the community of God, will be given a special place in the Lord's house and an immortal value:

> Let not the foreigner who has joined himself to the
> Lord say: "The Lord will surely separate me from his
> people"; and let not the eunuch say: "Behold, I am a
> dry tree." For thus says the Lord: "To the eunuchs
> who keep my sabbaths, who choose the things that
> please me, and hold fast my covenant, I will give in
> my house and within my walls a monument and a
> name better than sons and daughters; I will give them
> an everlasting name which shall not be cut off . . .
> these I will bring to my holy mountain, and make them
> joyful in my house of prayer; their burnt offerings and
> their sacrifices will be accepted on my altar; for my
> house shall be called a house of prayer for all
> peoples." Thus says the Lord God, who gathers the
> outcasts of Israel; I will gather yet others to him be-
> sides those already gathered.[44]

The application of this prophecy to the homosexual can be defended, because the term "eunuch" in the New Testament is used not only in its literal sense—i.e., those who have been physically castrated—but also in a symbolic sense for all those who for various reasons do not marry and bear children. For example, in Matthew 19:12, Jesus, discussing marriage and divorce, says to his apostles: "There are eunuchs who have been so from birth, and there are eunuchs who have been made eunuchs by men, and there are eunuchs who have made themselves eunuchs for the sake of the kingdom of heaven."[45]

The first category—those eunuchs who have been so from birth—is the closest description we have in the Bible of what we understand today as a homosexual. It should come as no surprise, then, that the first group of outcasts of Israel that the Holy Spirit includes within the new covenant community is symbolized by the Ethiopian eunuch. It is the Spirit who takes the initiative by leading Philip to the encounter with the Ethiopian eunuch of the Court of Candace. The eunuch believes in Christ as the Messiah and receives baptism and the Spirit and rides on into history "full of joy." The symbolism of the passage is quite obvious. The Holy Spirit takes the initiative in leading the new Christian community to include among its members those who were excluded for sexual reasons from the Old Testament community.

Later, when we consider natural law ethics, we will also consider whether, in the light of recent psychosexual discoveries, heterosexual images of what it means to be a man or a woman derived from the Bible can be uncritically accepted as God-given aspects of creation or whether it must be determined to what extent they are human creations open to serious theological criticism and possible change and development. We can conclude at this point, however, that a general consideration of human sexuality in the Bible leads to only one certain conclusion: those sexual relations can be justified morally which are a true expression of human love. Consequently, once all the cultural and historical circumstances are kept in mind, the only condemnation of homosexual activity to be found with certainty in Scripture is a condemnation of perverse homosexual activity indulged in by otherwise truly heterosexual individuals as an expression of contempt or self-centered lust and usually associated with some form of idol worship. In the Old Testament an attempt was made to desacralize human sexuality by removing it from the realm of the mysterious and impersonal forces of nature. In the New Testament an attempt was made to resacralize human sexuality by integrating it into the ideal context of free, interpersonal human love.

The positive ideal concerning the use of human sexuality proposed in the New Testament is the need all human beings are under to struggle to integrate their sexual powers into their total personality, so that their sexual drive can be totally at the disposition of their desire to achieve union in love with their fellow human beings and with God. There is a considerable body of evidence—the Hooker, Shofield and Weinberg and Williams studies, for example, which I will discuss further on—that many homosexuals have avoided the traps of promiscuity and depersonalized sex by entering into mature homosexual relationships with one partner with the intention of fidelity and mutual support.[46] By means of this relationship they have not only escaped promiscuity but have grown as human beings. They have learned to integrate their sexual powers in a positive way into their personality, with the result that these impulses become no longer a negative, compulsive, and destructive force, but an instrument within their control for the expression of human love. There does not seem to be a clear condemnation of such a relationship in Scripture; yet under these circumstances a homosexual relationship could possibly be interpreted as fulfilling the positive ideals of Scripture.[47]

3
Tradition and Homosexuality

The Appeal to Tradition

Many moralists buttress their claim to found the objective sinfulness of homosexuality on scriptural data with an appeal to tradition. "The Christian tradition has constantly accepted the view that homosexuality goes against the Christian understanding of human sexuality and its meaning."[1] While admitting that historical circumstances and methodological shortcomings have possibly led tradition into error on certain points, yet, Curran concludes, "there seems to be no sufficient evidence for such a judgment in the case of homosexuality." The natural law approach proposed by Aquinas "still seems to correspond to a certain human connaturality condemning homosexuality as wrong."[2] This "human connaturality" might be just that, but it is even more likely that it might be a cultural prejudice formed and fed by tradition itself. In fact, one can and should ask all the same critical questions of tradition that have been previously asked of the scriptural data, especially since that tradition had its primary origin in the scriptural data.

There are three principal sources to which explicit appeal is made in Western Christian tradition in support of its condemnation of homosexual practices. The first is the contrast in cultural mores between Greek and Hebrew culture. The early Christian community, primarily drawn from among the Jews of the diaspora, were inclined to see any variation of behavior in Greek culture as a deviation from the divine law given to Israel and as the inevitable breakdown of morality due to idolatrous practices. The second major source of the condemnation of homosexual practices was an appeal to the popular Stoic philosophical concept of nature, a concept which culminated in Aquinas's version of natural law. The third source, and in some respects the most important, since it was deemed to be a divine confirmation of the first and second sources, was the prevalent version of the Sodom and Gomorrah story. Let us begin our critical reflection on tradition with this third source.

The Homosexual Interpretation of the Sodom Story

As we have seen, the sin of Sodom was never interpreted in Old Testament times as being primarily sexual, to say nothing of involving homosexual practices; rather it is portrayed as a sin of pride and inhospitality. The first references to the sin of Sodom which indicate explicitly that that sin was of a sexual nature occur in the Palestinian apocrypha of the second century before Christ. In the *Book of Jubilees* XVI.5–6 we read:

> the Lord executed his judgment on Sodom, and Go-
> morrah and Zeboim, and all the region of the Jordan,
> and he burned them with fire and brimstone, and de-
> stroyed them until this day, even as (lo) I have
> declared unto thee all their works, that they were

wicked and sinners exceedingly, and that they defiled
themselves and committed fornication in their flesh,
and worked uncleanness on the earth. And in like manner God will execute judgment on the places where
they have done accordingly to the uncleanness of the
Sodomites, like unto the judgment of Sodom.[3]

In a later passage in the *Book of Jubilees* (XX.5–6) an
interesting parallel is drawn between the sin of the Sodomites and the sin of the giants:

and [Abraham] told [his sons and grandsons] of the
judgment of the giants, and the judgment of the Sodomites, how they had been judged on account of their
wickedness, and had died on account of their fornication, and uncleanness, and mutual corruption through
fornication.

The giants referred to here are the "sons of God" referred to
in Gen. 6:1–4 and the "angels" of 2 Peter 2:4 and Jude 6.
The "Watchers" of Jewish legend (*Enoch* VI–X; *Jub.*
VII.21f., X.5f.; *Test. Reub.* V.6–7; *Test. Naph.* III.5) are
represented as lusting after mortal women and descending
on earth to enjoy coitus with them. In the *Book of Jubilees*
VII.20–22 we read:

Noah exhorted his sons to . . . guard their soul from fornication and uncleanness and all iniquity. For owing to
these things came the flood upon the earth, namely,
owing to the fornication wherein the Watchers against
the law of their ordinances went a-whoring after the
daughters of men, and took themselves wives of all
which they chose; and they made the beginnings of
uncleanness.

It was from this unlawful intercourse that the Naphidim, or
giants, were born. The *Book of Jubilees* thus draws a

parallel between two occasions when illicit sexual conduct called forth the vengeance of the Almighty. These passages represent the first departure from the general tradition of Scripture by stressing the sexual character of the sin of Sodom; but that sin is still not indicated as homosexual in nature; rather, it is heterosexual and consisted in the commission of adultery and acts of gross sexual license and shameless promiscuity between men and women. As we have seen, some experts believe that both the scriptural passage dealing with Noah and the flood and the passage dealing with Lot and the rain of fire contain material from the Priestly tradition attacking ancient idolatrous practices concerned with seeking rain, practices which involved sexual orgies.

In a contemporary document, *The Testament of Naphtali* II.4–5, one of the *Testaments of the Twelve Patriarchs*, a Palestinian work of Pharisaic origin, we have the first indication of the sin of Sodom as homosexual in nature:

> recognizing . . . in all created things, the Lord who made all things, that ye become not as Sodom, which changed the order of nature. In like manner the Watchers also changed the order of their nature, whom the Lord cursed at the flood. . . .

Here the offense of both the Watchers and the Sodomites is said to have consisted in changing the "order of nature." Both committed a similar breach of a universal principle of order established by the Creator. The Watchers subverted the natural and evident order by the unlawful mingling in coitus of two incongruous elements, the angelic and the human. If we recall that in the Sodom story the visitors were angels, then the chief offense seems to be understood as a searching for unlawful commerce with an incompatible order of beings, whereas the sexual element is subsidiary in the mind of the author. This interpretation is supported by a New Testament passage, Jude 6–7, in which the evidence of these apocryphal texts can be detected:

> and angels which kept not their own principality, but left their proper habitation, he hath kept in everlasting bonds under darkness unto the judgment of the great day. Even as Sodom and Gomorrah, and the cities about them, having in like manner with these given themselves also to fornication and gone after strange flesh [*hetera sarx*], are set forth as examples suffering the punishment of eternal fire.

Once again the homosexual element is only incidental; the emphasis is upon the sexual incompatibility of the angelic and human orders rather than upon any particular type of coitus between persons of the same sex. Bailey concludes from this evidence that by the end of the first century A.D., though the sin of Sodom is still regarded as a transgression of order, there is also a perceptible emphasis of its homosexual implications. However, as the *Testament of Naphtali* gives evidence, this development began as early as the second century B.C. The concept of transgression of order adds a new element in a polemical addition to the *Testaments* during the period 70–40 B.C.: "and the daughters of the Gentiles shall ye take to wife, purifying them with an unlawful purification; and your union shall be like unto Sodom and Gomorrah." The reference here is to the mixed marriages so much abhorred by strict Jews. Since Sodom had also come to be associated with barrenness, the passage probably implies that union with Gentile women contracted in defiance of the law will be cursed with sterility.

The next step in this development can be traced to the "writing of Enoch," a lost work written in Hebrew. In the

Testament of Naphtali IV.1, we find this reference: "I have read in the writings of Enoch ye yourselves also shall depart from the Lord, walking according to all lawlessness of the Gentiles, and ye shall do according to all the wickedness of Sodom." R. H. Charles regards this passage as a loose adaptation of a passage from the *Book of the Secrets of Enoch*, a Hellenistic Jewish work based on the *Writings of Enoch*.[4] In *2 Enoch* XXXIV.2 among the lawless actions of the Gentiles is clearly indicated that of homosexual practices. Consequently by approximately 50 B.C. the interpreters of the *Testaments of the Twelve Patriarchs* began to regard the sin of Sodom as including homosexual practices. The clear connection that the *Testament of Naphtali* V.1 establishes between the "wickedness of Sodom" and the "wickedness of the Gentiles" is significant. This lends support to the possibility that the origin of the homosexual interpretation of the Sodom story can be explained by the Jewish reaction to a closer acquaintance with homosexual practices common in the Hellenistic world during the century preceding the Christian era.

Another passage from a later stratum of *2 Enoch* explicitly identifies the sin of Sodom with the pederasty of Hellenic society: "This place [the north region of the third heaven] is prepared for those who dishonor God, who on earth practice the sin against nature, which is child-corruption after the Sodomitic fashion. . . ." However, the first writings to identify the sin of Sodom with homosexual practices in general—the writings which probably had the most decisive influence on early Western Christian tradition—were those of Philo, dating from the middle of the first century A.D., and those of Josephus, from around the year A.D. 96. The first recorded instance of a homosexual coital connotation being clearly attributed to the Hebrew word *yādhá* in the text from Genesis occurs in Philo's *Quaest. et Salut. in Genesis* IV.31–37, where *yādhá* or *suggignomai* is interpreted as "servile, lawless and unseemly pederasty." The association of the wickedness of Sodom with the lawlessness of the Gentiles has become particularly associated with the pederasty of an alien and hostile culture.

In his work *De Abrahamo*, Philo reads all the evils of first-century Alexandria back into the story of Sodom in Genesis:

> The land of the Sodomites was brimful of innumerable iniquities, particularly such as arise from gluttony and lewdness. . . . The inhabitants owed this extreme license to the never-failing lavishness of their sources of wealth. . . . Incapable of bearing such satiety . . . they threw off from their necks the law of nature, and applied themselves to deep drinking of strong liquor and dainty feeding and forbidden forms of intercourse. Not only in their mad lust for women did they violate the marriages of their neighbors, but also men mounted males without respect for the sex nature which the active partner shares with the passive, and so when they tried to beget children they were discovered to be incapable of any but a sterile seed. Yet the discovery availed them not, so much stronger was the force of their lust which mastered them, as little by little they accustomed those who were by nature men to play the part of women, they saddled them with the formidable curse of a female disease. For not only did they emasculate their bodies, but they worked a further degeneration in their souls, and, so far as in them lay, were corrupting the whole of mankind.[5]

Most of the most prevalent myths and prejudices concerning homosexuality find expression here, such as the myth of effeminacy—the idea that homosexuals must either play the active-masculine role or the passive-feminine role in their relationships—the myth of corruption, and the myth of child abuse. Philo probably did not invent these myths but, as Bailey points out, was only expressing in vivid language a conception of Sodom and its offense which had gradually established itself among Jews of the diaspora during the preceding two centuries of their contact with Hellenic society.

In his *Antiquities* Josephus also clearly identifies the sin of Sodom with homosexual practices, and in particular with pederasty:

> About this time the Sodomites were proud on account of their riches and great wealth; they became unjust toward men and impious toward God. . . . They hated strangers, and abused themselves with Sodomitical practices. God was, therefore, much displeased with them, and determined to punish them for their pride.

This passage represents the first clear use of the word sodomy to describe homosexual practices. In still another passage from Josephus' *Antiquities* we read: "Now when the Sodomites saw the young men [the angels] to be of beautiful countenance, and this to an extraordinary degree . . . they resolved themselves to enjoy these beautiful boys by force and violence."

Although there are good grounds to believe that by the end of the first century A.D. the sin of Sodom had become widely identified, among the Jews of the diaspora, with homosexual practices, yet it is remarkable to note that rabbinical writings reflect scarcely anything of this development. The majority of the references to Sodom both in the Talmud and the Midrashim continue to stress the Old Testament themes of pride, arrogance, and inhospitality. The one exception to this is a midrash on Genesis: "The Sodomites made an agreement among themselves whenever a stranger visited them they should force him to sodomy and rob him of his money."[6] The writer implies that the most serious and reprehensible feature of the Sodomites' inhospitality was homosexual acts reserved for strangers and accompanied by violence and robbery.

When we turn to the Fathers of the Christian Church, there is no doubt whatever that they accepted without question that the sin of the Sodomites was their particular and inordinate addiction to homosexual practices, particularly pederasty, and it was for this reason that God punished them. Clement of Alexandria, for example, writes that the Sodomites had "through much luxury fallen into uncleanness, practicing adultery shamelessly and burning with insane love for boys."[7] John Chrysostom, in a homily to the people of Antioch, writes: "The very nature of the punishment was a pattern of the nature of the sin. Even as [the Sodomites] devised a barren coitus, not having for its end the procreation of children, so did God bring on them such a punishment as made the womb of the land for ever barren and destitute of all fruit."[8] Augustine in his *City of God* speaks of Sodom as "the impious city where custom had made sodomy as prevalent as laws have elsewhere made other kinds of wickedness."[9] In another work Augustine repeats Paul's theme in the Epistle to the Romans that homosexual perversion is itself a recompense for other offenses, since such acts are not only sins per se but also the penalties for sins. In the *Apostolic Constitution* we read: "Thou shalt not corrupt boys: for this wickedness is contrary to nature and arose from Sodom."[10] We should note a second factor entering into the picture with the writings of the Fathers, namely, the Stoic concept of sexual nature with its emphasis on procreation, leading to the judgment that homosexual practices were "contrary to nature." We shall deal with Stoic influences on Christian tradition later on.

Herman van de Spijker summarizes his study of the attitude of the Fathers of the Church on the subject of homosexuality with these words:

> The Fathers consistently rejected homosexual activity. The argument for this rejection was based on the order of creation and the Epistle to the Romans. Sodom is the cautionary example of the punishment to be expected or the clear sign of the lawlessness of such activity. . . . Although the fierceness of the condemnation can be better understood in terms of anti-Hellenic and apologetic motives, and although the Fathers speak mostly against the lust of pederasty and of perverted and self-perverting heterosexuals, yet implicitly they condemn all homosexual activity as contrary to the order of creation. We can conclude from both the biblical and the patristic heterosexual image of man that the Fathers had no understanding of the difference between homosexuality as a subjectively moral expression of love or as an egotistical expression of lust.[11]

The Development of Legal Tradition

A survey of Western Christian tradition concerning homosexual practices would be incomplete without a consideration of the treatment of these practices in Roman law, especially in the codifications of the Christian emperors Theodosius and Justinian, since these codifications exercised a very strong influence not only upon Western European systems of civil and criminal jurisprudence but also upon ecclesiastical law.

The *Lex Scantania* was the original Roman law directed against pederasty, but little is known about it. The next legal measure was the emperor Philip's law (A.D. 249) abolishing male prostitution. The *Lex Julia de adulteris* (ca. 17 B.C.) was probably extended by an interpretive process to include sexual acts committed with boys, a crime meriting capital punishment. For we read that on 30 December 533 the following law was included among the *Institutes* compiled by Tribonian at the emperor Justinian's request:

> In criminal prosecutions cases, public prosecutions take place under various statutes including the *Lex Julia de adulteris*, . . . which punishes with death (*gladio*) not only those who violate marriages of others, but those who commit acts of vile lust with [other] men.[12]

Thus Roman law was extended to include homosexual acts of all kinds, including those between consenting adults, and the death penalty was assigned.

The first law under the Christian emperors was promulgated on 16 December 342 by Constantius and Constans:

> When a man marries [and is] about to offer [himself] to men in a womanly fashion, what does he wish, when sex has lost its significance; when the crime is one which is not profitable to know; when Venus is changed into another form; when love is sought and not found? We order the statutes to arise, the laws to be armed with an avenging sword, that those infamous persons who are now, or who hereafter may be, guilty may be subjected to exquisite punishment.[13]

As Bailey remarks, it is difficult to know how seriously to take this edict. W. G. Holmes remarks that its curious phraseology "almost suggests that it was enacted in a spirit of mocking complacency."[14]

Fifty years later, on 6 August 390, another law was put forth by Valentinian II, Theodosius, and Arcadius:

> All persons who have the shameful custom of condemning a man's body, acting the part of a

woman's, to the sufferance of an alien sex (for they appear not to be different from women) shall expiate a
crime of this kind in avenging flames.[15]

This law is particularly notable because it prescribed the
penalty of burning, which was the most common criminal
punishment imposed upon sodomists in the Middle Ages
and has persisted at least nominally in some countries until
recent times.

Bailey was of the opinion that these earlier Roman laws
were never rigidly enforced. For by the year 538 Justinian
found it necessary to publish the first of his *Novellae* against
homosexual acts:

> since certain men, seized by diabolical incitement,
> practice among themselves the most disgraceful lusts
> and act contrary to nature; we enjoin them to take to
> heart the fear of God and the judgment to come, and to
> abstain from suchlike diabolical and unlawful lusts, so
> that they may not be visited by the just wrath of God
> on account of their impious acts, with the result that
> cities perished with all their inhabitants. For we are
> taught by the Holy Scriptures that because of like im-
> pious conduct cities have indeed perished, together
> with the men in them. 1 . . . For because of such
> crimes there are famines, earthquakes, and pestilences,
> wherefore we admonish men to abstain from the afore-
> said unlawful acts, that they may not lose their souls.
> But if after this our admonition any are found persist-
> ing in such offences, first, they render themselves un-
> worthy of the mercy of God, and then they are
> subjected to the punishment enjoined by the law. 2.
> For we order the most illustrious prefect of the Capital
> to arrest those who persist in the aforesaid lawless and
> impious acts after they have been warned by us, and to
> inflict on them extreme punishments, so that the city

and state may not come to harm by reason of such wicked deeds.[16]

The chief motive behind this law is clearly stated. Justinian sees homosexual practices as endangering the state, for they are liable to provoke the vengeance of God in the form of earthquakes, famine, and pestilence. We see here the influence of the homosexual interpretation of the Sodom story. Bailey finds the approximate cause of this legislation in the terrible earthquake and floods which in the year 525 devastated the cities of Edessa, Anazarba, and Pompeiopolis in the East, Corinth and Dyrrachium in Europe, while Antioch was destroyed by fire and inundations. In the year 543 a great plague swept through Constantinople. It was doubtless with this in mind that Justinian took occasion during the following Lent, on 1 March 544, to issue a new novella summoning to repentance those in particular whose homosexual practices might provoke other and possibly more dreadful consequences. In that novella he returns to the theme of Sodom:

1. For, instructed by the Holy Scriptures, we know that God brought a just judgment upon those who lived in Sodom, on account of this very madness of intercourse, so that to this very day that land burns with inextinguishable fire. By this God teaches us, in order that by means of this we may avert such an untoward fate. . . . Wherefore it behooves all who desire to fear God to abstain from conduct so base and criminal that we do not find it committed even by brute beasts.[17]

Justinian's treatment of homosexual practices became the *locus classicus* for civil legislation concerning this matter. An illustration of how pervasive and perduring that influence was is to be found in Blackstone's treatment of homosexual practices in his *Commentary on the Laws of England:*

> The crime against nature [is one which] . . . the voice
> of nature and of reason, and the express law of God,
> determined to be capital. Of which we have a special
> instance, long before the Jewish dispensation, by the
> destruction of two cities by fire from heaven; so that
> this is a universal, not merely a provincial, precept. In
> the Old Testament the law condemns sodomists (and
> possibly other homosexual offenders) to death as perpe-
> trators of an abomination against the Lord, while in the
> New Testament they are denounced as transgressors of
> the natural order and are disinherited from the king-
> dom of God as followers of the vile practices of the
> heathens.[18]

The first enactment of a Church council concerning homosexual practices occurred at the Council of Elvira in 305–6. This decree forbade admission of *stupratores puerorum* to communion even at death.[19] The decree of the Council of Ancyra in Asia Minor in 314 was extremely influential on the Church in the West, since it was frequently cited as authoritative in subsequent conciliar enactments against homosexual practices. Canon 17 concerns those "who either have been defiled or commit defilement with animals or males."[20] The council prescribes a variety of punishments dependent on the age and marital status of the perpetrator. Males, if married and over fifty, are to be admitted to communion only at the point of death. Basil of Nyssa in the year 375 in a letter to Amphilochius, bishop of Iconium, writes: "He who is guilty of unseemliness with males will be under discipline for the same time as adulterers."[21] Gregory of Nyssa in a canonical letter to Letoius, bishop of Melitene (ca. 390), explains the reason for treating sodomists the same as adulterers, namely, because both combine unlawful pleasures with the infliction of injury upon another.[22] Basil and Gregory both call for fifteen years of penitence and exclusion from the sacraments. In 693 Egica, king of Gothic Spain, in an opening speech to the Sixteenth Council of Toledo, urged the clergy to address themselves to curbing homosexual practices, and once again an implicit appeal was made to the Sodom story: "Among other matters, see that you determine to extirpate that obscene crime committed by those who lie with males, whose fearful conduct defiles the charm of honest living and provokes from heaven the wrath of the supreme judge."[23]

The most extensive set of enactments against homosexual practices during medieval times were the canons issued by the Council of Naplouse on 23 January 1120 by Baldwin II, king of Jerusalem, and Garmund, patriarch of Jerusalem.[24] On that occasion a sermon was preached in which all the ills that had befallen the Kingdom of Jerusalem as well as earthquakes, menacing signs, and the attacks of the Saracens were attributed to evil living. Consequently, the council enacted twenty-five canons against the sins of the flesh, four of which dealt with homosexual practices, and burning was prescribed for the impenitent. By the end of the twelfth century sodomy was a reserved sin which must be referred to the bishop or the pope for absolution.[25]

The penitentials (works on the sacrament of penance originating in the Celtic churches of Ireland and Wales) illustrate how the Church attempted to deal with homosexual practices. Their chief concern was to discriminate as fairly as possible between different kinds of acts according to their nature and circumstances and assign appropriate penances. The use and influence of the penitential spread to England, France, Germany, and even Italy and determined for five centuries the standards according to which

penance was administered. The most notable pronouncement on the subject of homosexual practices in the Middle
Ages was the *Liber Gomorrhianus* of Peter Damian, addressed in 1051 to Pope Leo IX.[26] In this work Peter
inveighs against the practice whereby the penitentials
distinguish between types of homosexual acts and assign
different penances. In particular he calls for the removal
from orders of any cleric found guilty of such acts. Leo's
response, *Nos Humanius Agentes*, is chiefly remarkable for
its emphasis upon the need for a sense of proportion and a
more humane approach to the question of homosexual
practices. He rebukes the harsh, unyielding spirit of Peter's
work, maintaining that not all those who engage in homosexual acts are equally sinful, and thus not all merit the
same ecclesiastical censure. He especially notes that it is
not necessary to depose a cleric from orders for this reason,
concluding: "And if anyone should dare to criticize or carp
at this decree of ours, let him know that *he* is in danger of
his orders."[27]

Consequently, as Bailey has demonstrated, the formation
of the Western Christian attitude to homosexual practices
underwent a cumulative process of development in which
many diverse influences played a part, the postexilic Jewish
reinterpretation of the Sodom story, pagan and Christian
developments of Roman law, the teaching of the Church
Fathers, the legacy of Church councils and synods, the
penitential system, and so on. By the end of the thirteenth
century, and especially with the writings of Aquinas, that
tradition was fully formed. The influence of the homosexual
interpretation of the Sodom story is evident in every strand
of that development. There was a tendency on the part of
civil officials to read into any disaster a divine judgment due
to homosexual practices. For example, with regard to the
wreck of the *Blanche-Nef* in 1120, in which the heir of
Henry I of England perished with a number of young

nobles, William of Nangis asserts that this was a divine punishment due to the fact that all were sodomists.[28] At the time of the Albigensian heresy there began a tendency to associate homosexual practices with heresy. Since the Albigensian heresy was also known as the Bulgarian heresy, the word *bougre* became associated with sodomy and remains in our present vocabulary as the word "buggery."[29] Bailey argues that although the Albigensians never advocated homosexual practices, their position that marriage was a state of sin gives some credence to the opinion that they had an easygoing attitude toward other forms of sexual activity. All too often unscrupulous politicians would make use of a charge of homosexual activities in order to defeat their political enemies. But it is notable that the Church itself never imposed capital punishment for this sin; rather, its emphasis was on repentance and rehabilitation. In fact the Church courts, by attempting to retain jurisdiction over this question, tried to protect the accused against the more severe punishments of the civil courts.

The ultimate culmination of legal injustice and persecution of the homosexual community in recent times occurred in Hitler's Germany. In 1936 Heinrich Himmler issued a decree which read: "Just as we today have gone back to the ancient German view on the question of marriages mixing different races, so too in our judgment of homosexuality—a symptom of degeneracy which could destroy our race—we must return to the guiding Nordic principle, extermination of degenerates." Orders were given that all homosexuals had to wear pink triangles in public, just as Jews had to wear a star of David. In 1937 the SS newspaper, *Das Schwarze Korps*, estimated that there were two million homosexuals in Germany and called for their extermination. Himmler gave orders that all homosexuals were to be sent to Level 3 camps—that is, death camps.

No one knows exactly how many homosexuals perished. The Austrian Lutheran Church places the number of homosexuals who died at no less than 220,000, the second largest group after the Jews. However, the injustice and the indignity did not end with the fall of the Nazi regime. After the war all other survivors of the concentration camps were treated generously in the matter of reparations. Homosexuals, however, were told that they were ineligible for compensation, since they were still technically "criminals" under German law. The survivors could not even publicly protest, since they had to keep their homosexual identity secret for fear of further discrimination.[30]

The Anomalies of Tradition

In dealing with tradition, it must not be forgotten that the readily available documents which lend themselves to historical interpretation, such as the Bible, law codes, the enactments of councils, and so on, are really only the surface of that tradition—"the proximate or immediate determinants," as Bailey calls them. Underlying these documents are various deep-rooted socio-psychological factors which have come to conscious awareness only in recent times and still await full and careful examination. Speaking of scriptural tradition, Neale Secor remarks:

> One might continue the corrective process by delving into the rather late times when the Genesis traditions were formed for a greater appreciation of the then cultural needs of the monogamous agrarian family unit, the real fear of Canaanite and other apostate idolatrous sexual-religious practices, the primitive reverence for the semen, and the biological misunderstanding regarding the conception and birth processes.[31]

G. Rattray Taylor in his book *Sex in History* attempts to bring out some of the culturally conditioned attitudes on sexuality.[32] He finds a universal phenomenon in cultures based on a patriarchal principle. These cultures always tend to combine a strongly subordinationist view of women with a repression and horror of male homosexual practices, whereas cultures based on a matriarchal principle are inclined to combine an enhancement of the status of women with a relative tolerance for male homosexual practices. Taylor concludes that the tradition of the Christian West has been fundamentally "patrist." This may help to explain certain striking anomalies from an ethical viewpoint in that tradition, anomalies which have affected profoundly our laws and public opinion in regard to homosexual practices.[33]

One of the most remarkable of these anomalies is the almost complete disregard of lesbianism in the various documents we have examined. Although the Holiness Code, for example, explicitly condemns under penalty of death male homosexual practices and female bestiality, no mention is made of female homosexual practices. Apart from a disputed reference to unnatural female acts by Paul in Romans 1:26, there is no reference to female homosexuality in Scripture and scarcely any in all the other documents of tradition.

There is a marked tendency, as we have seen, in all the sources of tradition to condemn sodomy in terms of a man "playing the role of a woman" with another man, or using another man "like a woman." As Bailey remarks, this has been looked upon in tradition as the degradation not so much of human nature as of the male as such.[34] If there is a certain message in the narratives of Sodom and Gomorrah and of the Crime of Gibeah, as McKenzie remarks, it is the belief of the time in the absolute respect that should be shown the male and the relative lack of concern for the female. Or from another perspective, one begins to suspect in a careful reading of the documents of tradition that human nature and maleness were frequently identified emotionally, if not consciously, in the popular mind. To stimulate or encourage or compel another to simulate the passive coital function of the female represented a perversion intolerable for a society organized according to the theory of the essential subordination of woman to man, a society which particularly valued male aggressiveness and dominance. Consequently, as Bailey remarks, a man who acted "like a woman" was treated as one who had betrayed not only himself but his whole sex, dragging his fellow men down with him in his voluntary disgrace.

The premise of male superiority also helps to explain the curious disparity between the moral judgment passed upon heterosexual moral offenses on the one hand and homosexual offenses on the other. There is a tradition of referring to homosexual practices as "the most heinous" of all sins. This tradition seems to take its rise in the story of Joseph (Gen. 37:2), where Joseph is reported to have brought back a "bad report" of his older brothers to his father. The Vulgate translates the passage as "accusavitque fratres suos apud crimine pessimo." Although there is no basis whatsoever in the Bible for reading into this passage an accusation of homosexual practices, yet the term *crimen pessimum* became associated with these practices.

The tradition of male superiority also helps explain why in the popular view female prostitution, fornication, and even adultery are frequently treated with less contempt than homosexual practices. These immoral actions at least proclaim the essential virility of their perpetrators. Every effort at legal reform concerning male homosexual practices brings forth the irrational contention that male homosexuals do more harm to society than a person who seduces a wife or husband, breaks up a marriage, assaults or injures a young girl, begets and abandons an illegitimate child, etc.

And the more severe legal penalties testify to the effectiveness of that contention.

Another reason for the distinction traditionally made between male and female homosexual practices is the observation that only male homosexual practices involve the emission of seminal fluid. There has been a definite influence on Western sexual attitudes and on traditional moral theology derived from a reverence for human male semen. This reverence had its origin in an ignorance of human physiology and the conception and birth processes. Because there was no knowledge of the female process of ovulation, women were traditionally believed to be merely the incubators in which male seed was deposited. Clement of Alexandria spoke of the male semen as *"met oligon anthropon*—something almost or about to become a man."[35] The idea that the male semen at emission was almost human controlled sexual theory until the biological investigations of human physiology in the sixteenth century. Even Galen spoke of there being no difference between "sowing the womb and sowing the earth."[36]

Despite the advances in our knowledge of these processes, the ancient tradition continues to influence our ideas of sexual conduct and morality until the present day—for example, the moral attitude to male masturbation. Bailey believes that the reverence for the male seed as "almost human" was undoubtedly responsible in no small measure for the fact that society has always tended to reprobate and punish homosexual practices of males while more or less ignoring those of females.[37]

Although our ignorance of birth processes has been a thing of the past for several centuries and the emancipation of women has made definite strides, something of this deep-seated but irrational view of women remains today to influence the attitude of men in general toward the homosexual male. As we shall see, Dr. George Weinberg believes that the real psychological crisis in our culture remains male homophobia.[38] The evidence from tradition suggests an interesting connection between the status of women and the status of the male homosexual that remains to be explored. Even celibate priests are frequently themselves victims of an unconscious homophobia. When John Harvey did a survey of Catholic priests concerning their attitude toward male homosexuals who might seek their advice, he discovered:

> Some betrayed an emotional revulsion even to a pastoral discussion of inversion, quoting St. Paul that such things should not be mentioned among us. Others dismissed the subject with an abrupt declaration that nothing can be done for inverts and the writer was wasting his time. Still others assumed a harsh attitude of bitter condemnation.[39]

The lesbian's practices, on the other hand, do not involve any lowering of a privileged social or personal status. Consequently, they can be relatively ignored by a society in some respects fundamentally androcentric and homophobic. Bailey concludes:

> It might perhaps be well for us frankly to face the fact that rationalization of sexual prejudices, animated by false notions of sexual privilege, has played no inconsiderable part in forming the tradition which we have inherited and probably controls opinion and policy today in the matter of homosexuality to a greater extent than is commonly realized.[40]

4
Tradition and Human Nature

The Influence of Stoicism

One important aspect of Western Christian tradition remains to be examined, namely, the influence of Stoicism, especially its interpretation of the natural law as regards sexual ethics. Underlying the attitude of the early Church to homosexual practices there was, as we have seen, the belief that they were specially condemned by God in the destruction of Sodom and Gomorrah. Nevertheless, such practices were generally denounced mainly on the grounds that they were in themselves "contrary to nature."

The first such reference to nature, as we have seen, occurred in Paul's Epistle to the Romans. The *Apostolic Constitutions* speaks of "abhoring as unlawful, and that which is practiced by some contrary to nature, as wicked and impious."[1] Tertullian writes: "All other frenzies of lusts which exceed the laws of nature and are impious toward both bodies and the sexes we banish, not only from the threshold, but also from all shelter of the Church, for they are not sins so much as monstrosities."[2] John Chrysostom is particularly emphatic in denouncing homosexual practices as unnatural. Commenting on Romans 1:26–27, he observes that all genuine pleasure is according to nature; the delights of sodomy, however, are an unpardonable insult to nature and doubly destructive. They jeopardize the race by deflecting the sexual organs from their primary procreative purpose, and they sow disharmony between men and women, who are no longer impelled by their physical desires to live peacefully together.[3] Michel Spanneut, an authority on the influence of Stoicism on the Church Fathers, maintains that the moral writings of nearly all the Fathers of the Church in the first two centuries of the Christian era "were dominated by the popular Stoicism of the milieu in which that Christian generation lived."[4]

Stoic philosophy was primarily a moralism. Seneca defined philosophy as "recta vivendi ratio."[5] The fundamental Stoic axiom was to "live according to nature." Life according to nature was understood as submission to the divinely appointed order of the world. Nature itself was identified, however, not with instinct but with reason: "To the rational animal the same act is according to nature and according to reason."[6] God, in Stoic philosophy, was understood as reason, or *logos*, diffused through the cosmos. Reason, as "soul of the world," was given a definite biological interpretation. The law of nature was identified with the biological laws governing the physical universe. Thus the rational law of nature represented God's material presence in the universe as cosmic biological reason. To conform to the physical laws of nature was simultaneously to achieve union with the divine. "Live with the gods. And he lives with the gods whoever presents to them his soul accepting their dispensations and busied about the will of God, even that particle of Zeus, which Zeus gives to every man for his controller and governor—to wit, his mind and reason."[7]

The principal virtue of the wise man was understood as ataraxy, or apathy—a life of indifference. In practice Stoic ethics was largely a fight against the passions or affections. These passions—pleasure, sorrow, desire, and fear—were considered irrational and, consequently, unnatural. All forms of passion, even pity and love, were to be eliminated as irrational. The process of achieving a state of indifference was understood as a process of eliminating the influence of affection on human behavior, so that behavior would be totally controlled by reason and completely independent of all externals, even of other persons.[8] In order to escape chance and its capricious happenings, such as the death of a loved one, man must render himself indifferent to all exterior results of his actions, judging them only in terms of their interior effect, which is to be found in the intention. As Spanneut remarks: "The notion of apathy, applied to God, to Christ, and especially to the Christian, received special emphasis. Baptized from the time of Origen, it was used by all the writers [of the early Christian period], particularly in the treatises on anger, and became the ideal of the monk, the basis of his contemplation."[9] Clement of Alexandria devotes an entire chapter of the *Pedagogue* to the connection between good and reason, evil and irrationality.[10] Many of the Christian martyrs—Justin, for example—quote extensively from Stoic sources concerning the virtue of indifference. The Fathers of the Desert appeal to Stoic indifference as the foundation of asceticism. Basil uses the same theme in his writings concerning monastic asceticism.

Hand in hand with the virtue of indifference, the Stoic philosophers stressed a doctrine of rational determinism, according to which everything that happens in the world happens with an ineluctable necessity. "If the gods have determined about me, they have determined well; for it is not easy to imagine a deity without forethought. And as to doing me harm, why should they have any desire toward that? For what advantage would result to them from this, or to the whole which is the special object of their providence?"[11]

Particular emphasis was placed on the triumph over all fears, especially the fear of death. The Stoics denied the immortality of the individual as such; impersonal reason alone is eternal. Thus the only rational response to death was to become detached from life, including one's own. "Be not perturbed, for all things are according to the universal, and in a little time thou wilt be nobody and nowhere, like Hadrian and Augustine."[12] One should learn to value one's existence rationally; that is, only in terms of the positive contribution one can make to the totality. Since the spirituality of the early Church evolved in response to the needs of the martyr, the emphasis on indifference and triumph over the fear of death received particular emphasis.

Along with stress on mind and reason went a dualistic depreciation of the body, both as the seat of the irrational passions and as the contingent element in man. "Nam corpus hoc animi pondus ac poena est, premente illo lorgetur, in vinculis est."[13] Death is to be welcomed as the release of the mind from the chains of the body.

Seneca advised a daily examination of conscience in which one would tote up all the positive and negative aspects of one's existence precisely in terms of one's being able to make a positive contribution to the totality. The truly wise man will become indifferent to life itself. The day he sees his continuance in existence as more of a negative than a positive value, he will be ready to take his own life. The Stoic hero is pictured as cutting his own veins in a warm bath while discoursing in noble indifference about reason to his admiring friends. Thus Seneca himself, in obedience to Nero's command, opened his veins in A.D. 65.

But to persevere in his indifference, the key point in Stoic doctrine was to "never fall in love," that is, never to form a real attachment to anyone. Marcus Aurelius points out that to fall in love is to open yourself up to every misery and to lose all tranquility of soul; for lovers necessarily desire personal immortality both for their loved ones and for themselves. But such a desire is irrational. Love for another must only take the form of "love for the virtue of which this person is an example." Similarly, in his treatise on friendship Thomas Aquinas holds: "The happy man will need these virtuous friends inasmuch as he seeks to study the virtuous actions of the good man who is his friend."[14]

Consequently, when the Stoics turn to sexual conduct it should come as no surprise that no consideration whatsoever is given to interpersonal love. Rather, stress is placed on the rational end of sexual activity as this end can be read in the biological laws of nature which are one with the will of God. Accordingly, the only rational motive for undertaking sexual intercourse is procreation. Zeno remarks that "cannibalism, incest, and homosexuality are not wrong in themselves," his reasoning being that moral evil pertains to the human will and intention. These actions become wrong because no purely rational motive can exist for such practices.[15]

Stoicism and the Church Fathers

In order to understand the attitude of the Fathers of the Church toward homosexual activity, we must place it within the context of their attitudes on women and on sexuality in general. The early Fathers of the Church tended to accept Platonic and Stoic body-soul dualism. As Emil Brunner notes: "Through Platonic-Hellenic mysticism the idea penetrated into the early Church that the sexual element as such is something low and unworthy of man . . . an idea which . . . is in absolute opposition to the biblical idea of creation."[16] The Fathers frequently repeat Aristotle's dictum that "the woman is a mutilated male" and agree with his position that the male is by nature superior and the female inferior; the one rules and the other is ruled.[17] There is a tendency to identify the male principle with the soul and the female principle with the body. Woman is naturally subject to man because in man the direction of reason is greater. This went hand in hand with a sexual interpretation of original sin, with Eve symbolizing all women as the evil protagonist.

In fact, Saint Augustine went so far as to identify all sexual attraction and pleasure with sin. This is Augustine's portrayal of what sexual intercourse exclusively for the purpose of procreation would have been like before man sinned:

> Without the seductive stimulus of passion, with calmness of mind and with no corrupting of the integrity of the body, the husband would lie upon the bosom of the wife. . . . No wild heat of passion would arouse those parts of the body. . . . The semen would have been introduced into the womb of the wife with the integrity of the female organs being preserved, just as now with the same integrity being preserved, the menstrual flow of blood can be emitted from the womb of a virgin. . . . Thus not the eager desire of lust, but the normal exercise of the will should join the male and female for breeding and conception.[18]

Gregory of Nyssa in his turn, in his work *On the Creation of Man*, accepted the androgyne myth of Plato's *Symposium*, namely, that primal human beings were bisexual. Gregory believed that the male-female severance was a result of sin and a punishment for sin. As a consequence all sexual desires are a vice and have their origin in corrupted nature. John Scotus Erigena, in the ninth century, accepted Gregory's position that humans as the perfect image of God were originally without sexual differentiation and that sin was the cause of the differentiation which ensued.[19] In such a climate of opinion it should come as no surprise that Marcion, for example, should refuse to accept into the Church anyone who refused to renounce all sexual relations permanently.

The purely rational end of sexual behavior, procreation, is continuously stressed by the Church Fathers when they are dealing with sexual morality and marriage. One can clearly see the influence of popular Stoic philosophy in the insistence on reason rather than on the sacramental aspect of marriage. Clement, for example, emphasizes the irrationality of seeking only pleasure in marriage.[20] Justin Martyr reflects popular Stoicism when he writes: "We [Christians] do not enter marriage for any other reason than to have children."[21] Jerome quotes the saying of Sextus with approval: "He who loves his own wife ardently is an adulterer."

Aquinas and Stoicism

Thomas Aquinas was the only great scholastic theologian to discuss the subject of homosexual practices in any detail. Albert the Great, in a short reference, gives four reasons why this is the most detestable of practices: it proceeds from a burning frenzy; it has a disgusting foulness; those addicted to it seldom succeed in shaking off the vice; and, finally, it is as contagious as any disease, rapidly spreading from one to another.[22]

In contrast to that of Albert, Thomas's treatment is calm and dispassionate.[23] As in the case of the Fathers, we must place Thomas's treatment of homosexuality in the context of his treatment of women and of sexuality in general. Woman, he held, was "the inferior workman who prepares the material for the skilled artisan, the male."[24] He theorizes that since every child born should be male, because the effect should resemble its cause, there must be some etiological explanation for the birth of the inferior female. Such a birth, he claims, need not necessarily be the result of some intrinsic factor—a "defect in active power" or an "indisposition of the material"—but may sometimes arise from an extrinsic accident. He quotes the Philosopher (Aristotle) to the effect that "a moist south wind helps in the generation of females, while a brisk north wind helps in the generation of males."[25] Thomas's attitude toward women is best expressed when he says of Eve: "She was not fit to help man except in generation, because another man would have proved more effective help in anything else."[26]

Concerning human sexuality in general, Aquinas rejects John Scotus's position that sexual differentiation as such is due to sin, but he agrees with Augustine's Stoic view that all sexual pleasure is the result of sin.[27] The Stoic influence is evident in the fact that Aquinas deals with the subject of homosexuality in the course of his treatise on the cardinal virtue of temperance. He identifies the vice contrary to this virtue as lust, whose essence is "to exceed the order and mode of reason where venereal acts are concerned." Any act which is not consistent with the proper end of venereal acts, namely the generation and education of children, necessarily pertains to the vice of lust. The lustful man desires not human generation but venereal pleasure, and it should be noted that this pleasure can be experienced by indulging in acts which do not issue in human procreation. It is precisely this which is sought in the sin against nature.[28]

Thus the first grounds for Thomas's condemnation of homosexual practices is his belief that they necessarily represent an inordinate selfish seeking of venereal pleasure; and, as we have seen, Thomas believed that all such pleasure is the result of sin. What we should note with interest is that there is no mention in this passage of a third possible motive for venereal acts, whether heterosexual or homosexual, besides either lust or procreation—namely, the possibility that they might be an expression of genuine interpersonal love. There is no reason to assume that Aquinas had any more awareness than had the Church Fathers of the homosexual condition. Rather, it is almost certain that in his reference to homosexual practices he is assuming that these are merely sexual indulgences undertaken from a motive of lust by otherwise heterosexual persons. This is the conclusion drawn by Joseph McCaffrey in his study of Aquinas's treatment of homosexuality. Having rigidly subordinated the rational and, therefore, moral use of sex in general to one end—procreation—Aquinas assumes that homosexual acts, since they cannot serve that purpose, must be motivated necessarily and exclusively by a drive toward sexual pleasure.

In a response to an objection that if no one is injured by homosexual activities, there is no sin against charity, Aquinas points out that the order of nature is derived from God. Consequently, any contravention of that order is necessarily "an injury done to the Creator."[29] Thus the most fundamental objection Aquinas had to homosexual practices was identical to that of the Stoics: they cannot serve the exclusive divine purpose governing the use of all human sexuality, the end of procreation. It would seem that Aquinas, like his Stoic predecessors, never even considered the possibility that human sexual behavior, even in a heterosexual context, never mind a homosexual one, could be morally justified as an expression of human love.

In one relatively unknown but important passage in his *Summa Theologica*, Thomas speaks of homosexual practices as capable of being "connaturale secundum quid."[30]

He asks the question, When is pleasure "according to nature"? He distinguishes between those pleasures that are according to human nature specifically as rational—such as the "contemplation of the truth"—and those pleasures which humans have in common with other animals—such as "venereal activity" (*veneorum usus*). But, he continues: "In the case of both types of pleasure it can happen that what is unnatural simply speaking can be connatural in a certain situation. For it can occur that in a particular individual there can be a breakdown of some natural principle of the species and thus what is contrary to the nature of the species can become by accident natural to this individual [*per accidens naturale huic individuo*]." Among other examples of this, Thomas explicitly mentions male homosexual activity (*in coitu masculorum*). Unfortunately he never explores this distinction further.

To deal exclusively with the passages in which Aquinas speaks explicitly of homosexual practices is somewhat un-just to his influence upon the consequent development of sexual ethics. Although Aquinas himself did not apply his new insights to practical ethical issues, he did lay the philosophical foundation for a personalist ethics. It was not until he reversed the act-potency relationship of Greek philosophy with his central idea of a real distinction be-tween essence, or nature, as potency and existence as act that a philosophical foundation was laid for understanding human beings as positively individual and unique and, therefore, incapable of being legitimately totally relativized to the ends of the species from an ethical viewpoint. Further, Thomas opened up the possibility of conceiving human nature not as a static given, but as a dynamic teleological process of growth and development. This made possible an understanding of ethical norms as ideal goals governing the development of personal community, rather than just biological nature. But this development had to await the work of philosophers true to the spirit, if not the letter, of Thomistic philosophy. It was not until the rise of modern personalist philosophies of human subjectivity and freedom that an appropriate methodology for an ethical study of human sexuality in a personalist context became available.

Homosexual Activity and Procreation

Many moral theologians grant that the older Catholic approach to sexual morality inordinately placed all the emphasis on the biological and physical aspects of the sexual act, ignoring the interpersonal context in which the act takes place. "The procreative aspect becomes the primary and sometimes the only purpose of sexuality."[31] However, these same moralists are of the opinion that one must maintain some connection between the personal and the procreative aspects of human sexuality: "The joining together of the love union and procreative aspects does appear to be the meaning of human sexuality and marriage. There seems to be a strong presumption in favor of such an understanding which cannot be overturned without grave reason."[32]

When, therefore, they come to the specific question of homosexual behavior, these same theologians appeal to this necessary and indissoluble connection between procreation and human sexuality as another reason for the condemnation of homosexual activity:

> The position of the hierarchical magisterium in the Roman Catholic Church would argue that every single act of sexual intercourse must be open to procreation. Obviously, such an approach gives one a strong rule and criterion to use in condemning homosexual acts or other seemingly errant forms of sexual behavior.[33]

This is by no means as obvious a conclusion as many believe. The Church's attitude toward the ends of marriage has undergone a definite development. Beginning with an early insistence, under Stoic influence, on the exclusive end of procreation, at a later stage the Church began to stress procreation as the primary end, but granted the existence of secondary ends, namely the mutual love and fulfillment of the marriage partners. The Church as traditionally recognized the moral goodness of heterosexual relations between a married couple incapable of having children; this despite the heavy emphasis of tradition that procreation must be the primary aim of all sexual activity. For example, Pope Pius XI in his encyclical *Casti Connubii* (No. 59) writes:

> Nor are those considered as acting against nature who in the married state use their right [to sexual intercourse] in the proper manner, although on account of natural reasons either of time or of certain defects, new life cannot be brought forth. For in matrimony as well as in the use of matrimonial rights there are also secondary ends such as mutual aid, the cultivation of mutual love and the quieting of concupiscence which husband and wife are not forbidden to consider as long as they are subordinated to the primary end and so long as the intrinsic meaning of the act is preserved.[34]

From the moment the Church granted the morality of the rhythm method, for example, as a natural form of birth control, and justified sexual activity as still fulfilling the "secondary" aims of mutual love and fulfillment, there was a serious reason to reconsider the traditional position that all homosexual activities are necessarily wrong on the ground that they cannot lead to procreation. In a relatively overlooked passage of the same encyclical, *Casti Connubii*, the mutual love between the partners is recognized in its own right as the "primaria matrimonii causa et ratio":

> The mutual inward moulding of husband and wife, this determined effort to perfect each other, can in a very real sense, as the Roman Cathechism teaches, be said to be the chief reason and purpose of matrimony, provided matrimony be looked at not in the restricted sense as instituted for the proper conception and education of children, but more widely as the blending of life as a whole and the mutual interchange and sharing thereof.[35]

In their treatment of marriage in the document Pastoral Constitution on the Church in the Modern World, the Council Fathers at Vatican II go a step further in this development by dropping all reference to primary and secondary ends. As Robert McAfee Brown comments:

> The document . . . goes far beyond the traditional teaching that the procreation and education of children are the primary ends of marriage. Thanks to the interventions of such men as Cardinals Léger and Suenens, the document stresses the importance of conjugal love. Sexual love between men and women is clearly distinguished from "the dispositions of lower forms of life"— where one has a suspicion it often used to linger in the thought of earlier moral theologians. Pure conjugal love "involves the good of the whole person." In such statements the lie is given to the notion that sex in marriage is evil, or only a concession to concupiscence, or valid only for procreation.[36]

The Church continues to condemn any voluntary separation of the coequal purposes of sexual behavior, procreation and mutual love. However, such an argument against vol-

untary separation would be applicable to the homosexual
only if one refuses to accept the psychological data concerning the homosexual condition and persists in viewing all
those who involve themselves in homosexual practices as
remaining free to choose heterosexual relationships. The
genuine homosexuals' situation is more comparable factually to that of a heterosexual couple incapable of having
children than, for example, to the situation of those who
practice birth control, since it is not through a free choice
within their control that homosexuals eliminate the possibility of procreation from their sexual life. Yet there is a
considerable body of evidence that those homosexuals who
have limited their sexual expression in an ethically responsible way have by that means achieved what Pius XI
indicates as the "chief reason and purpose of sexual love
within marriage looked at in a wider context "as the
blending of life as a whole and the mutual interchange and
sharing thereof."

Human Nature and Homosexuality

One all-important problem remains. Even granting that
mutual love and fulfillment is a coequal natural end of
human sexuality as such, there seems to be a lingering
doubt that this end could possibly justify homosexual activities, since these activities seem so obviously to involve a
perversion of the biological function of the sexual organs.
As we have seen, the phrase "against nature" has retained
its meaning from its Stoic origin as "contrary to reason."
One learns the purposes of nature by an impersonal and
objective reading of the biological law governing the sexual
operations of the human body. However, this understanding of nature represented in fact a rejection of what is
unique in human nature as such, namely, the personal
realm. Consequently, it negates any possibility of under-

standing human sexual activity within the specifically human dimension of interpersonal love.

Humans emerge from the impersonal forces of nature precisely as self-aware and free. What is specific about human nature is not some quality which is common to all the species, such as reason, but the fact that "every individual is more than the species."[37] It is this personal uniqueness of every individual which forms the necessary basis for the possibility of human love. A loving action, even if it takes the form of a sexual gesture, must be directed to the other as unique, an end in himself or herself. To treat another person merely as a means to an end that lies outside the person represents a failure to love that person as unique.

From this personalist viewpoint an overemphasis on procreation can be seen as leading potentially to a seriously immoral and dehumanizing form of sexuality. Modern consciousness has been sensitized by the movement for women's rights to the fact that to understand the female exclusively in a functional manner as "bearer of children" is a depersonalizing and, therefore, immoral attitude. Such an emphasis can be seen as in conflict with the Gospel emphasis on the respect and love due to one's fellow human as person. As we have seen, a general consideration of scriptural data concerning sexual behavior leads to only one certain conclusion: those sexual relations can be justified morally which are a true expression of human love. The call of the Gospel is not one of conforming passively to biological givens; rather, that call is to transform and humanize the natural order through the power to love.

The overemphasis on nature, reason, and law in tradition has seriously falsified the moral question of sexual behavior in the minds of many people. The average person has associated and confused the question of the *morality* of sexual conduct with the question of its objective *legal* status. The reason for this confusion is, in part, that one finds a very easily applied objective norm: sex before marriage is wrong; sex after marriage is right. The difficulty of this norm can be easily perceived if we begin with the question of the moral quality of sexual conduct within marriage. The wife who withholds sex with a view to negotiating a fur coat is acting immorally; she is behaving like a prostitute, even if a legal prostitute. And the husband who uses his wife as a convenient instrument of masturbation, seeking exclusively his own egotistical pleasure, is immoral and remains so even if the act is open to the possibility of procreation. From these examples it should be obvious that there is something more to the moral quality of sexual behavior than the purely objective legal question of marriage, or even the objective rational question of openness to procreation. Something else ought to be present; and that something else is love. Are you using your sexual powers as a means of expressing your love? Are you centering your existence in the one you love and seeking his or her fulfillment in what you are doing? The human conforms to the divine image revealed in Christ not by acting in an impersonal, rational way, but by acting from a motive of love.

Human Freedom and Human Sexuality

It is obvious that the traditional moral theologians understood human sexual behavior as rationally determined by biological instinct. Thus the only freedom they believed men and women to have in the sexual realm was the freedom to conform to the rational end built into biological instinct, procreation, or to thwart that end. However, we have become progressively aware in recent times that human sexuality, like all human reality precisely as human, participates in the radical freedom that is ours. In forming their respective judgments, many moralists seem to ignore the rather obvious fact that human sexuality is not a totally instinctive and, therefore, determined phenomenon. Whatever participates in human freedom cannot receive its total explanation in terms of causal determinacy. Rather, it can be adequately understood only in terms of ideal goal or purpose. We are freed from a deterministic *vis a tergo* precisely because we are able to project ideal goals and, consequently, allow these ideals to be the ultimately determining factor in our behavior.[38]

We do not find it "contrary to nature" that humans have taken the hands which biological evolution provided as grasping instruments and employed them in the ideal creative pursuits of wielding a brush or a pen. Nor do we find it contrary to nature that the mouth with its teeth, tongue and lips, obviously intended by nature for eating, should be used in order to communicate through speech and song humanity's most intimate aspirations. Nor should we find it any less according to nature, if men and women should use their sexual organs, designed by nature for procreation, in order to give the most intimate expression to their drive for union in love with their fellow human beings.

How, then, does our freedom enter into the formation of human sexual orientation? We are born male or female, biologically speaking: but biological givens never determine human behavior precisely as human. We become "men" or "women" through a free human process of education. What it means to be a man or woman in any given society or culture is a free human cultural creation. Every culture has created its ideal sexual-identity images for the masculine or feminine role. Successful cultural adaptation represents the process whereby the young, unconsciously for the most part, adapt themselves to the prevalent cultural image and expectations which go along with their biological identity.

More often than not in the past, these cultural identity images contained seriously dehumanizing factors. It is only in recent times that humanity has become aware that these images are not predetermined either by God or nature. As long as the cultural process remained unconscious there was little awareness of the role human freedom played in the formation of these images. Because these images were considered as either divine or psychological givens or taboos and their true character as free human constructs was not recognized, there was no hope of liberation from their destructive and antihuman elements. Primitive cultures tended to sacralize the prevailing images, seeing them as given by the gods. However, as Thomas Driver convincingly argues in his article "Sexuality and Jesus," over against the pagan gods and the pagan religions Jesus appeared as the great neutralizer of the religious meaning of sex; and, thus, as humanity's liberator from narrow sexual taboos mistakenly identified as divine imperatives:

> I believe that the construction of a Christian ethic of sex cannot be properly attempted as long as one retains the mythology of sexuality that grew up in the ancient religions, is perpetuated in the new ones, and from which Jesus as the Christ would liberate us.[39]

Since the sexual-identity image which concretizes heterosexual relations at any point in human history is a human and not a divine creation, theologians who absolutize the man-woman relation as the "divine image" in human beings are guilty of raising a human creation to the level of an idol. The task of the theologian, true to the spirit of Jesus in the New Testament, should be to liberate humanity to "the glorious liberty of the Sons of God," precisely by undertaking a critical theological investigation of sexual-identity images. As we have seen, the primary God-given ideal goal of human sexual development is that we should fashion cultural identity images that make it possible for human beings to achieve the fullness of a true personal relationship of sexual love in the process of conforming to the images provided by culture.

A growing body of evidence derived from cultural anthropology, sociology, and psychology indicates that in the learning process whereby humans conform to the sexual-identity images of their culture, a certain percentage, approximately one out of ten, fail to acculturate themselves successfully according to the acceptable heterosexual pattern. This appears to be a consistent and universal cultural phenomenon, the same in all cultures and in all periods of history.[40] Since it is the divine plan that humans should freely construct their cultural identity images, and since it seems to be a universal phenomenon that a certain percentage of humans do not necessarily conform to the accepted heterosexual pattern, no matter how heavily conformity to that pattern is sanctioned by society and the Church, I see no reason to assume a priori that the human who emerges from that unconscious learning process as a homosexual is somehow alienated from God's plan or in conflict with nature's design. On the contrary, it would seem more reasonable to assume that the homosexual is part of the divine plan and has an intrinsic role to play in human society. What that role may be will be the object of our inquiry in the second part of this work.

Paul Lehmann, in his work *Ethics in a Christian Context*, makes the point that the concern of a Christian ethics should be to relate the intimate reality of human sexuality in all its forms to the freedom and integrity of human wholeness: "What is called for in Christian sexual ethics is an approach which accents both the fundamental importance of the sexual act for the humanization of man and the setting in which that humanization of man is a concrete and achievable reality."[41] Kimball-Jones suggests that for the true homosexual such a setting can only exist in an encounter with another person of the same sex. Such an encounter is "the only sexual setting in which 'the humanization of man' can begin to become 'a concrete and achievable reality' for the homosexual."[42]

Homosexual love, although incapable of procreation, is certainly not doomed to fruitlessness. Many homosexual couples love, and would gladly adopt, children if the law would permit it. Apart from this, it is certain that by means of a homosexual love many humans have been liberated to a truly spiritual fertility which otherwise would have been impossible. And as DeKruijf remarks in a different context: "In the New Covenant it is given to anyone to be fertile in the new people of God through a love which surpasses even marital love in value and therefore in fertility."[43] We shall treat of the potentially positive aspects of homosexuality later on. First we must investigate the contribution of the human sciences to our moral understanding of homosexuality.

5

The Human Sciences and Homosexuality

The Use of Scientific Data

As Curran points out, there are two questions concerning the use of empirical data derived from the human behavioral sciences: the substantive question, which has to do with a search for the meaning of homosexuality in terms of the human sciences such as psychology, sociology, psychiatry, anthropology, cross-cultural studies, etc.; and the methodological question concerning the way in which such data should influence and be incorporated into moral judgment.

He rejects, on the one hand, the methodological position of Karl Barth, which would "exclude all human wisdom as helpful to the Christian ethicist, and depends exclusively on revelation."[1] On the other hand, he equally rejects Milhaven's methodology "of relying exclusively on communal experience which in this case is preeminently the findings of psychology and psychiatry."[2] In contrast to Milhaven, Curran emphasizes the dynamic and progressive character of moral judgment, which always is concerned with what ought to be in contrast to the present experience

109

of what is. "Present experience too easily forgets the prophetic aspect of Christian teaching, which corresponds with an eschatology which negatively criticizes the present in the light of the future."[3]

Since the human experience which enters into ethical judgment must be total, it must relate to the full reality of the world around us, including our relationship to God and to our fellow humans. Such an experience can never be reduced exclusively to the data of the behavioral sciences, since "these scientific disciplines have a perspective which can never be totally identified with the human perspective."[4] The final human moral judgment must be a synthetic and creative judgment which, while incorporating the data of the human sciences, must relativize all these data in terms of the total human perspective.

Granting the value of this methodological statement, the real difficulty arises when we consider the substantive contribution of the human sciences to an understanding of the meaning of human homosexuality. Some moralists believe that a telling argument for the validity of the traditional condemnation of homosexual practices comes from the data of the human sciences, the majority of which, Curran claims, "seem to point to the fact that human sexuality has its proper meaning in terms of the love union of male and female."[5]

What we are witnessing in the writing of many moral theologians, especially in the area of sexual ethics, is a shift in the basis for understanding what constitutes human nature. Whereas, as we have seen, traditional sources based their understanding of sexual nature primarily on an objective biological function, the modern theologian tends to seek primary evidence for what is true to human nature from psychological and sociological data. Consequently, most modern condemnations of homosexual practices are based in so-called psychological or sociological data.

Promiscuity and Homosexuality

The claim is frequently made on the basis of scientific data that homosexual acts represent a failure in full human development and that homosexual practices are necessarily psychologically destructive for the parties involved. Curran, for example, insists that those who argue in favor of homosexuality "fail to come to grips with the accepted fact that *most* homosexual liaisons are of the 'one night stand' variety." Consequently, there is no sexual union expressive of loving commitment to one another. "No one can deny that there are many stable relationships, but these do not clearly constitute the majority of the cases."[6]

The scientific data that Curran adduces in support of his statement that most homosexual liaisons are promiscuous derive from a reference in a footnote to a sociological study, "Homosexuality: The Formation of a Sociological Perspective," by Simon and Gagnon. He quotes these sociologists as writing: "These data, then, suggest a depersonalized quality, a driven or compulsive character quality, to the sexual activity of many homosexuals, which cannot be reckoned as anything but extremely costly to them."[7] Curran himself acknowledges, however, that there are "many stable homosexual relationships" and lists the authors of a number of recent scientific studies (Clara Thompson, Evelyn Hooker, Wardell Pomeroy, etc.) who indicate the hitherto unsuspected numbers of such successful liaisons.[8]

These same authors establish excellent reasons why these stable liaisons must remain hidden and, consequently, why accurate statistical data concerning the stability of homosexual liaisons is for all practical purposes difficult, if not impossible, to obtain. Thus there can be no certain scientific data to justify a clear conclusion that "stable relationships are not a majority." In view of widespread premarital activity, prostitution, marital infidelity, the increasing divorce rate (which one survey claims is rapidly approaching the fifty percent mark), etc., one wonders what specific data could be offered to prove the existence of a lesser degree of infidelity and depersonalized and compulsive sexual activity among heterosexuals. Whenever and by whomever sexual promiscuity is indulged in, one has to do with a neurotic, unhappy, and compulsive form of sexuality. The real moral miracle the data does give witness to is that despite every obstacle that society and the Church have placed in the way of homosexual relationships, many have succeeded in maintaining a high degree of stability and have provided a truly human companionship and fulfillment.

As for the statement "Those who argue in favor of homosexuality have failed to come to grips with the problem of the transitory nature of many homosexual liaisons," just the opposite is the truth.[9] The majority of authors dealing with the problem recognize and establish beyond serious doubt that the primary reason for this negative quality in many homosexual liaisons is the guilt and self-hatred which so many homosexuals tend to introject as a result of the judgment passed on them by society. As Dennis Altman observes:

> Like the black, the homosexual suffers from a self-fulfilling stereotype. Tell people long enough that they are inferior, and they will come to believe it. Most of us are niggers because we believe that we are in large part what society constantly brands us as; in response we come to exhibit the characteristics that justify our stigma. There are a large number of neurotic, unhappy, compulsively promiscuous homosexuals whom one might well regard as "pathological." This pathology is, however, the result of social pressures and the way they have internalized these, not of homosexuality itself. If people are led to feel guilty about an essential

part of their own identity, they will in all likelihood experience considerable psychological pressures.[10]

But even if we grant for the sake of argument that the majority of the homosexual's liaisons are promiscuous, this does not establish a rational grounds for the condemnation of homosexuality as such, but only of promiscuity. If it should happen that the data in a given society proved that the majority of heterosexual contacts were of a one-night-stand variety, would the conclusion follow, then, that heterosexual activities in themselves are sinful? Obviously one is assuming some unproven intrinsic connection between homosexuality and promiscuity. The fact remains that if even only one homosexual liaison can be proven to have been an expression of genuine human love and fidelity, then the existence of such an intrinsic necessary connection has been effectively disproven.

It does not take much imagination to understand how much heterosexual activity would tend to be dehumanized and compulsive if heterosexual liaisons were considered illegal and criminal by the state and the effect of sin by the Church. As we have seen, the insistence on the objective sinfulness of all homosexual relationships is precisely the type of moral thinking that psychologically destroys the ability of many homosexuals to enter into a permanent and fruitful relationship. The only certain substantive conclusion that follows from the scientific data is the terrible cost in terms of human suffering and degradation that has followed on the mistaken moral judgments and prejudices of the past which still are invoked to support the prejudices of the present.

Psychiatry and Homosexuality

One school of psychiatrists maintains that homosexuality in all cases represents a mental disease. A proponent of this position is Irving Bieber in his work *Homosexuality: A Psychoanalytic Study*. Isadore Rubin, in a discussion guide for SIECUS, reports that although there is no unanimity among specialists, the most commonly held opinion is that *all* homosexuals are mentally ill or neurotic. Edmund Bergler, in his book *Homosexuality: Disease or Way of Life*, defines homosexuality as

> a neurotic distortion of the whole personality. . . .
> There are no healthy homosexuals. The entire person-
> ality structure of the homosexual is pervaded by the
> unconscious wish to suffer. This wish is gratified by
> self-created trouble-making (psychic masochism) . . . he
> is an emotionally sick person.[11]

Many experts challenge this extreme position of some psychiatrists. They point out, first of all, that this group arrives at its conclusion as a universal judgment, not from experience but by means of an implicit invalid speculative argument. Assuming the sex drive as such to be the total economic content of the personality and defining hetero-sexual adjustment as the ideal and exclusive goal of uncon-scious personal development, they are forced to conclude a priori that all homosexuality represents a fixation at, or regression to, an immature stage of development. Irving Bieber begins with exactly the same assumption as the natural law ethicians: "We assume that heterosexuality is the *biologic* norm, and that unless interfered with all individuals are heterosexual."[12] Further, most psychiatrists tend to deal in the practical order only with those homo-sexuals who have severe neurotic disorders or personality conflicts, and almost never deal with the hidden majority who have managed more or less to escape severe emotional disturbance because of their condition. As one expert ob-served: "When clinicians speak of homosexuality, they are speaking of a very particular type of neurotic interaction, rather than a type of sexual behavior."[13] This observation is borne out by a statement in the introduction to Bergler's book: "All psychoanalytic theories assume that adult homosexuality is psychopathologic and assign different weights to constitutional and experiential components."[14]

Still another, and apparently larger, group of psychiatrists seems to take a middle position. Freud himself was the first clinician to suggest that homosexuality as such does not inherently constitute an emotional illness.[15] As Louis Crompton points out:

> When to such names as Freud and Krafft-Ebing, one adds those of Frank Beach, Harry Benjamin, Evelyn Hooker, Wardell Pomeroy, Alfred Kinsey, Robert Lindner, Judd Marmor, Michael Shofield, Thomas Szasz and Ernest van den Haag, as well as the Wolfenden Committee, the most distinguished government group ever to undertake a study of the subject, it is obvious, to say the least, that the sickness theory does not command the universal acceptance in scientific world which many assume it does.[16]

Many authors argue that the emotional disturbances which frequently accompany the homosexual condition are primarily the result of social pressures. These disturbances are usually not found in those cultures where homosexual behavior is socially acceptable.[17]

Still other authors point out that the neurotic traits ascribed to homosexuals are the same for any individual who identifies him- or herself with a persecuted minority. John Cavanaugh concludes his study of this question with the following statement:

1. Homosexuality is not a disease per se.
2. Deviant sexuality, including homosexuality, is the

result of a personality or character problem in which
the sexual orientation of an individual becomes fix-
ated at an early age.

3. Homosexuality may be a symptom of neurosis or
   psychosis, but in such cases it represents the individual's reaction to society or society's reaction to
   the individual.[18]

Kimball-Jones concludes his survey of the various opinions
of psychiatrists with this observation:

> While in each of these representative views homosexu-
> ality is seen as constituting a *psychiatric abnormality*,
> it is in no instance seen as inherently constituting a
> *serious and debilitating mental illness*.[19]

There are experts, however, who challenge the judgment
that homosexuality necessarily represents psychiatric abnormality. Wainwright Churchill, for example, points out
that there obviously are homosexuals who are homosexuals
because of their interpsychic conflicts. Their homosexuality
originates in such conflict and is maintained by it. However, any type of sexual behavior—homosexual, heterosexual, or autoerotic—can become associated with psychopathologic trends. When homosexuality is associated with
pathology, it tends to become compulsive; the individual
tends to use sexuality as a means of coping with anxiety,
much as the alcoholic uses alcohol. Churchill contends,
however, that clinicians in their diagnosis of *all* homosexuality as psychiatric abnormality have ignored the existence
of evidence coming from cross-cultural and cross-species
investigations. As one advances in the scale of evolution,
sexual behavior progressively loses its instinctual determination and more and more takes on the nature of learned
behavior. Among more advanced mammals, homosexual

behavior becomes more frequent. Explanations of adult homosexual practices in terms of complexes rooted in various childhood conflicts seem to have little or no applicability to these forms of homosexual behavior:

> To imagine for example that a baboon becomes positively conditioned to homosexual stimuli as a result of a pathological relationship with a "close-binding-intimate" mother or the result of some other complex is little less than ridiculous.[20]

Churchill testifies, however, to the psychological normalcy of many of his homosexual patients:

> This author wishes to go on record as one clinician among a multitude of others who has had the opportunity to interview, and, in several cases, to become acquainted with homosexual males who meet with every reasonable standard of mental health in their relationships with themselves and with others.[21]

Only in recent times has any effort been made to study those individuals who live relatively discreet, stable, lawabiding, constructive, and socially useful lives as homosexuals. Yet it is this group which may, perhaps, constitute the largest proportion of those engaging in homosexual practices. Perhaps the most important study done to date in America on the "well-adjusted" homosexual was that of Evelyn Hooker published in the New York Council of Churches report *Foundations for Christian Family Policy* (1961). Hooker sought out as her research subjects those homosexuals "who did not seek psychiatric help and who led relatively stable, occupationally successful lives." When the results of tests administered to this group were compared to those of tests administered to a like group of

heterosexuals, psychologists found great difficulty in determining who were the homosexuals, and in many cases
found "no evidence of any demonstrable pathology."
Hooker quotes a fellow clinician's conclusions:

> Homosexuality is not a clinical entity, but a symptom
> with different meanings in different personality set-ups.
> An overt homosexual way of life can play a construc-
> tive or destructive role in the personality. It may be
> the best type of human relation of which a person is
> capable, and as such is better than isolation. . . . Or it
> may be an added destructive touch in a deteriorating
> personality. In no case will it be found to be the cause
> of the rest of the neurotic structure—the basic origin of
> neurosis—although after it is established, it may con-
> tribute to the problem.[22]

A similar comparative study conducted by Michael Shofield
in England, *Sociological Aspects of Homosexuality*, supports Hooker's observations.

The Trustees of the American Psychiatric Association, in
their meeting of 15 December 1974, by a unanimous vote
ruled that "homosexuality" shall no longer be listed as a
"mental disorder" in its official nomenclature of mental
disorders. Formerly the Association's list of mental disorders included it as a "sexual deviation." The category of
homosexuality is now replaced by "sexual orientation disturbance," which is described as follows:

> This category is for individuals whose sexual interests
> are directed primarily toward people of the same sex
> and who are either disturbed by, in conflict with, or
> wish to change their sexual orientation. This diagnostic
> category is distinguished from homosexuality, which by
> itself does not necessarily constitute a psychiatric dis-
> order. Homosexuality per se is one form of sexual be-

havior and, like other forms of sexual behavior which are not of themselves psychiatric disorders, is not listed in this nomenclature of mental disorder.

Kimball-Jones concludes from his survey of opinions concerning the psychological nature of homosexuality that "there is far too little evidence available at the present time to decide one way or the other whether or not homosexuality is inherently a psychiatric abnormality."[23] This conclusion is important, as we shall see, from the moral viewpoint, since it precludes any universal condemnation of homosexual practices as morally wrong based on so-called "reliable scientific evidence" that they are necessarily universally destructive of personality.

John Milhaven, for example, attempts to argue on the basis of psychological evidence that homosexuality is a mental disease, that all homosexual relations are necessarily destructive of both parties and, therefore, ultimately immoral. Milhaven agrees that the Christian who lives by the new morality bases all his moral judgment and his life on

> something positive though general: the absolute divine command to *love*. Facing the question of homosexual behavior they would say: "God has laid down no specific and absolute prohibition of homosexual behavior. But He and I want absolutely one thing: that I live a life of love."[24]

Love is not just a question of feeling; experience teaches the honest person that some affectionate impulses lead to actions which in the long run hurt very badly the person he or she loves. Love, then, must be understood as "the free determination, commitment of a man or woman to further the good of a certain person." Milhaven admits that this is an old principle; its newness has to do with an *exclusive* reliance on experience rather than on a priori laws. However, since any one individual's experience of homosexuality is extremely limited, we must turn to the experience of the community; we must turn "to those who have extensive critical experience, preeminently the psychologists, psychiatrists and analysts." As a consequence, Milhaven makes use of the testimony of members of that group of psychiatrists and psychologists who, as we have seen earlier, hold the extreme position that homosexuality represents universally an "arrest of personality growth, stunted development, disturbed personality." Although he grants that these conclusions are not scientifically certain and other psychiatrists and psychologists dissent, nevertheless Milhaven sees this conclusion as the "most reliable experience in our community at the present time." He draws the following conclusion from this evidence:

> A man having genuine love for himself and others will refrain, in his behavior, from expressing and deepening particular feelings when the evidence on hand indicates strongly, if not with absolute certainty, that the feelings are profoundly immature and disordered. Consequently a Christian moving in the spirit of the new morality condemns homosexual behavior more severely than one using traditional arguments. . . . According to the Christian, moved only by love, relying on the experience of the community, homosexual behavior is wrong in that it frustrates *the man himself*. It fixates him at a stage far short of the full emotional and sexual development of the "being man" who is God's glory.[25]

It is obvious that there is a great need for further research and study in this area. But it is equally obvious that there is no communal experience or prevalent psychological evidence to justify Milhaven's conclusion. Since the available scientific evidence leads to no necessary and universal conclusion, nor even to a high degree of certainty, there is room left here for a cautious discernment in each individual case as to the effect a homosexual relationship is actually having on the personalities of the individuals involved.[26]

The Controversy among Psychiatrists

A few words of critique from a moral viewpoint should be written about the so-called scientific data derived primarily from one school of psychiatrists and psychologists that is frequently invoked by moralists to buttress their condemnation of homosexuality. As we have seen, this group defines homosexuality a priori as abnormality. Accepting the Freudian dogma that the sexual drive is the total economic content of the human psyche, heterosexual development is defined as the normal mature stage of development of the psyche. Moralists should note that such a dogma represents a pansexualism which precludes any recognition of a truly interpersonal dimension to human relations that in any way transcends the purely instinctive sexual drive. Such a dogma, since it divorces sexuality from its interpersonal context, deprives the moralist of any right to convert purely psychiatric data based on this dogma into moral judgment.

Further, psychiatrists deal exclusively with that portion of the homosexual community who consider themselves psychologically ill and, as a result, seek psychiatric help. They seldom, if ever, come into contact with those homosexuals who are living happy and fulfilled lives and who, since they do not consider themselves ill, never seek the aid of a psychiatrist. The frequently heard comment "I've never met a happy homosexual" says more, perhaps, about the speaker than it does about the homosexual community.

Many psychiatrists manifest a very unscientific zeal in their effort to "cure" homosexuals. The relation between a willingness to change and success in therapy has led some clinicians to advocate what from a Christian point of view is a morally reprehensible procedure. Bergler, for example, speaks of "mobilizing any latent feelings of guilt."[27] What he seems to be advocating is a deliberate effort to increase the guilt feelings and self-hatred of the patient. Bieber, who goes along with this type of practice, reports only twenty-seven percent of his patients were cured under optimum conditions.[28] One wonders what happened to the other seventy-three percent who left therapy unconverted but burdened with false guilt and shame concerning their incurable condition. To continue to hold out the false hope of a "cure," in the light of almost total failure to truly effect a cure, is morally reprehensible; for nothing can be more destructive psychologically than to hold out a false hope to an already disturbed person. Connected with the issue of false hope is the danger of false guilt in the case where analysis fails to change sexual orientation. The great stress some clinicians place on the a priori condition, on the patient's part, of a will-to-change as a necessary factor for the success of therapy could lead many into further depths of self-accusation and despair. For if therapy should fail, as it usually does, patients could easily draw the false conclusion that failure was due to a fault of their will, for which they are morally responsible.

Notice should be taken here of another form of therapy which has received some publicity in the popular press, namely, behavior therapy based on a stimulus-response version of learning theory. The experiments reported consisted of, in one case, "injecting an emetic mixture subcutaneously" and showing the patient pictures of nude males while he is feeling distress, then administering testosterone while showing pictures of nude females.[29] Still another form used electrical shock in the same context. There is a serious moral problem concerning this therapeutic method, reminiscent of the type of medical experiment carried on in Nazi concentration camps. The effort involved here of trying to bypass normal human consciousness and free response in order to change patterns of response and consequent behavior could easily result in a deterioration of the entire human personality and undermine any future possibility of personal growth in the basic human factors of freedom and responsibility. Although one may end up with someone capable of copulating with the opposite sex, that action would, perhaps, no longer be a human action expressive of love.[30]

Fortunately, there seems to be a growing awareness in the scientific community of the false scientific pretensions as well as the antihuman and immoral attitude of some psychologists and psychiatrists. Thomas Szasz, for example, in his work *The Manufacture of Madness*, writes about the "great ideological conversion from theology to science," which redefined sin as sickness and moral sanction as medical treatment. "This change from a religious and moral to a social and medical conceptualization and control of personal conduct affects the entire discipline of psychiatry and allied fields. Perhaps nowhere is the transformation more evident than in the modern perspective on so-called sexual deviations, and especially on homosexuality."[31] Szasz accuses his fellow psychiatrists of involving themselves in a program of social control that has nothing to do with genuine scientific medicine. They arrive at this position by pretending that social conventions are identical with nature, and by confusing the question of disobeying a traditional personal prohibition with mental illness. "They establish themselves as agents of social control and at the same time disguise their primitive interventions in the semantics and social trappings of medical practice."[32]

Clearly, Szasz maintains, the question the psychiatrist is posing when he speaks of homosexuality as illness concerns not the traditional concept of illness, but what moral or social significance contemporary culture attaches to the homosexual's behavior.

> Psychiatry's preoccupation with the disease concept of homosexuality conceals the fact that the homosexuals are a group of medically stigmatized and socially persecuted individuals. The noises generated by their persecution and their anguished cries of protest are drowned out by the rhetoric of therapy. It is heartless hypocrisy to pretend that physicians, psychiatrists or "normal" laymen for that matter, really care about the welfare of the mentally ill in general, or the homosexual in particular. If they did they would stop torturing him while claiming to help him. But this is just what reformers— whether theological or medical—refuse to do.[33]

Szasz sees the modern medicine man playing the same role vis-à-vis the homosexual community that the Inquisition did of old. He points out that for many decades the insinuation of homosexuality about one's adversaries has been an accepted strategy in American political life. However, if the psychiatrist really believes that homosexuality is an illness like any other, why does he not protest when it is used as a means of social degradation and political disqualification?

Szasz's conclusion is that psychiatric opinion about homosexuality is not a scientific proposition but a medical prejudice. In fact, Bieber carries that prejudice to the absurdity of classifying bachelorhood itself as a form of mental illness: "Failure to marry in either sex is the consequence of the fear of it. There is increasing recognition that bachelorhood is symptomatic of psychopathology."[34] One can only wonder what treatment (i.e., punishment) he would prescribe for the celibate priest or religious? Another psychiatrist, Robert Lindner, concludes that the psychiatric opinion concerning the homosexual as mentally ill reveals

> the same hostility for the invert and his way of life and the same abhorrence of him as a person that has been the tradition in Western society. That we now employ such terms as "sick" or "maladjusted" to the homosexual appears to me to make little difference so far as basic attitudes and feelings are concerned. As a matter of fact, I suggest that precisely these designations reveal the ugly truth of our actual animus toward homosexuals and the sham of modern social-sexual pretensions; for in the current lexicon such words reflect the nonconformism of their referents—and nonconformism is the major, perhaps the only, sin of our times.[35]

As Dr. George Weinberg suggests in his book *Society and the Healthy Homosexual*, there is a serious problem leading to considerable pathological consequences which should concern psychologists and psychiatrists; that problem is not homosexuality as such but homophobia.[36] The disease of homophobia consists in an attitude held by a majority of homosexuals themselves. "It is not surprising that the homosexuals themselves often suffer from the conventional attitudes of revulsion and anger toward things homosexual. In their case the problem is even more serious than elsewhere—the attitude is a condemnation of self."[37] Weinberg believes that the essential issue is not whether one is homosexual but how the person handles his or her homosexuality. Consequently, a major task for therapists should be to determine why some people regarded as deviants remain tormented while others are able to go on and live successful lives.

Even if a person is a heterosexual, however, a homophobic prejudice is certain to be harmful to him or her also. For such persons deprive themselves not only of homosexual experience, which they truly do not want, but of all else they connect with homosexuality. Weinberg observes that most men who loathe homosexuals have a deadly fear of abandonment to passivity: "The surrender of control signifies to them a loss of masculinity, and their demand for control produces narrowness."[38] Yet the ability to be passive is essential to all learning experience. Further, they also feel under tremendous pressure to be the aggressor in all fields of life, especially in sexual activity. What remains to be explored is how the homosexual community, by liberating the heterosexual community from its homophobia, can help to liberate us all to a fuller and more human life.

Despite the exaggerations of some therapists, granted that he or she has some positive understanding of the homosexual and is free from the crippling effects of homophobia, the therapist can be an indispensable help to the individual homosexual. The person who merely fears he or she may be a homosexual, or is attracted to the homosexual community, should explore every avenue toward the achievement of heterosexual capacities and relationships. This advice should be given independent of what one's moral judgment may be concerning homosexual relationships. If there is any hope of heterosexual adjustment in terms of psychological counseling, that escape from the difficulties of homosexual life should be explored. We shall deal at greater length with the question of heterosexual adjustment later on. However, even when there is no hope of heterosexual adjustment, therapy can still be a great benefit to many genuine inverts. A good counseling relationship can help them to self-acceptance and, consequently, open up the possibility of healthy and positive human relationships. [Author's note: I have changed my opinion on this matter. For my current thinking, see appendix 1, p. 201.]

Part 2

6
Toward a Positive Approach of Moral Theology

The greater part of both moral and psychological thinking concerning homosexuality tends to be prejudiced at its source, because it begins with a questionable presupposition. That presupposition, frequently explicit, maintains that the heterosexual condition is somehow the very essence of the human and at the very center of the mature human personality. Among moral theologians we have seen this at work in the assumption that heterosexual orientation is identical with the divine image in humanity. We met the same presupposition in a new context operative in at least one school of psychologists, represented by Irving Bieber, who begins his book *Homosexuality: A Psychoanalytic Study* with the statement: "We assume that heterosexuality is the biologic norm, and that unless interfered with all individuals are heterosexual."

Such an assumption effectively blinds the investigator to any evidence that a homosexual relationship can be a truly constructive and mature expression of human love, inasmuch as it holds that by definition mature and moral sexual love is heterosexual. As a consequence the only avenue of investigation open to anyone operating within this prejudicial viewpoint is to examine the etiology of homosexuality, searching out presumed causes of deviation from the biological and/or moral norm in faulty parental relations or in some constitutional causal factor. Further, this presupposition leaves only one course of action open to society, i.e., to do everything in its power to prevent homosexuality or, failing in this, to suppress all homosexual expression and seek a cure for its victims. In other words, society must treat homosexuals as carriers of a social and psychological disease to be handled in an analogous fashion to any physical disease, especially if it is considered contagious.

The Teleological Perspective

One can begin to detect, however, the beginnings of a totally different and more hopeful orientation of thinking in recent literature. The fruitful question is not "from whence" homosexuals came, but where they are going—or, better, to what purpose do they exist? As Pierre-Claude Nappey places the question:

> However much we may relativize the notion of a sexual norm and however much we may personalize the ethical exigency on which it is based, we are still not shedding any light on the reputedly obscure question of *why* homosexuality exists. . . . The question is not whether a certain type of behavior is excusable owing to the particular circumstances of the individual concerned, but whether it is an integral part of the much vaster behavioral pattern of the collectivity and whether it contributes in some way to its proper functioning.[1]

The peculiar importance of this question lies in the fact, as we have seen, that human sexuality participates in the radical freedom of the person. Whatever participates in human freedom can only be understood adequately in terms of ideal goal or purpose. Consequently, it is only by also posing the question *why*, for what purpose, that we can hope to arrive at an adequate understanding of the human phenomenon of homosexuality. For only by finding the answer to the teleological question can we detect in what sense homosexuality could be part of the divine plan and what intrinsic role it has to play in human society. As Nappey observes:

> Homosexuality must be seen . . . as corresponding to a definite finality. My own feeling is that not only is it possible for homosexuality to be of equal value with heterosexuality in individual cases, but that it has over-all significance and a special role to play in the general economy of human relations, a role that is probably irreplaceable.[2]

I believe no more urgent task faces the moral theologian than the difficult and complex undertaking of determining that finality. For on its discovery depends both the ability of the homosexual to accept himself or herself with true self-love and understanding and the ability of the hetero-sexual society to accept a homosexual minority, not just as objects of pity and tolerance at best, but as their equals capable of collaborating in the mutual task of building a more humane society.

The Positive Contribution of the Homosexual Community

What, then, is the collective role of the homosexual minor-ity in human society? And under what circumstances can that potential contribution become a reality? We have, perhaps, a clue to what that role is if we consider for a moment the frequently dehumanizing and depersonalizing role that prevailing sexual-identity images play in our culture. Dr. Harry Gershman, dean of the American Institute of Psychoanalysis, summarizes the objectionable stereotypes as follows:

> Men in our society are supposed to be strong, tough, assertive, objective, courageous, logical, constructive, independent, unsentimental, unemotional, aggressive, competitive, diligent, disciplined, level-headed, controlled, practical, promiscuous and persuasive. Women, in turn, are supposed to be weak, passive, irrational, emotional, empty-headed, unassertive, subjective, illogical, dependent, fitful, devoted, self-effacing, impractical, artistic and receptive.[3]

Commenting on these stereotypes, Dr. Eleanor Yaknes observes that gender identity is "the result of programming. Aside from the different physiology and anatomy, and vive la différence, I cannot think of any characteristic that is uniquely the property of either sex."[4] However, God help the man who may display a quality which society presupposes belongs exclusively to women, or vice versa.

An even more serious consequence follows if we assume that these heterosexual identity images constitute the total mature content of the human personality. For this results in the tendency to understand the human individual as essentially partial and incomplete. No human person is seen as complete in himself or herself, but only as essentially dependent on the other for his or her completion. The insights derived from the women's movement have rendered us all sensitive to the depersonalized and unequal status of women in our culture. And since man usually achieves his own identity in his relation to woman, he in turn also suffers a depersonalized and partialized self-image. Thus the consequence of identifying with the heterosexual identity images proffered by our society is that the only type of heterosexual relationship that remains possible is a type of master-slave relationship, wherein the male seeks to dominate and the female seeks to be dominated. It is precisely this understanding of direct personal relationships between the sexes as necessary and inescapable that led Hegel to despair of solving the problem of human unity on the personal level, and to seek that solution on the political level in the unifying concept of citizen. Marx turned to class identity to escape the same dilemma. There is no need to detail here how the inevitable frustration and dependence that result from this image leaves all of us open to all forms of exploitation, both economic and political. Once one grasps the limitations imposed by the prevailing images, it is hardly surprising that a certain percentage of individuals fail to be acculturated successfully.

True Christian love, even married love, can exist only between persons who see themselves as somehow total and equal. Christian love must be love out of fullness and not out of need. It is not only the complementariness of the other sex that attracts, as Nappey observes:

> It is also the fact that while I sense that complementarity I can at the same time sense that here is a being who is whole and entire in himself (or herself) and, although endowed differently than myself, worthy of standing beside me and entering my life as an equal.[5]

It should be obvious that the stereotypes mentioned above negate any possibility of such a personal relationship for any heterosexual who takes them seriously.

The homosexual community has, perhaps, a special role to play in liberating the heterosexual community to a fuller understanding of themselves as persons by being an organic challenge within society to the partial and dehumanizing aspects of these sexual-identity images. Psychoanalysts maintain that all humans are basically bisexual, and that the normal process of becoming heterosexual involves a homosexual stage in which the child learns to identify with the parent of the same sex. The homosexual stage in the development of human sexuality has a narcissistic function. It is precisely this element of narcissism to which many moralists turn to buttress their moral condemnation of homosexuality, interpreting it in moral terms of selfishness. J. Edgar Brun, for example, makes this statement: "We may not be able to regard true inversion as a willful betrayal of the ordained social order, but the driving force of narcissism which is inevitably present in it feeds a selfishness which can always destroy the dignity of human nature."[6] Such a moral judgment makes sense only on condition that one makes the sexual content of interpersonal relationships their total economic content. Homosexual love seen as an interpersonal relation can be just as selfless and other-centered as heterosexual love; in fact, since it escapes the debilitating effects of the heterosexual identity images, perhaps it has a better chance to form the basis of a genuine interpersonal love. As Eugene Kennedy observes:

> Is it really too horrendous to believe that a homosexual may, according to the modality of his sexual adjustment, be reaching successfully out of himself and toward another person in his sexual activity? Is it not possible that his effort to move out of himself and toward the other is the difficult-to-read sign of genuine growth on his part? In other words, homosexuality, even if it is not human expression at its full term, may be a forward movement for the lonely and isolated individual who breaks out of his narcissistic self-concern.[7]

The narcissistic function of the homosexual stage is viewed by some psychologists as having a positive function in human sexual development:

> Thanks to that function, every individual of whatever sex can learn to love himself sufficiently in order to reach the point where he will be led to take an interest in things other than himself. This normal and legitimate dose of narcissism, this quantum of homosexuality, is what makes it possible for one human to be attracted to another.[8]

Nappey sees here not only a question of individual psychology but of global, collective psychology. He sees, as a consequence, the homosexual community as playing the role of objectifying a necessary stage in human development. If the day should come when it became possible to suppress all homosexual tendencies, so that the homosexual could disappear from the face of the earth, we would then face the danger of removing a creative catalyst for the progressive development of sexual relations toward a fuller and more human reality:

> If heterosexuals honestly wish to see the perfect integration of persons and of the sexes, if they honestly hope to see the establishment of the best possible conditions for the fulfillment of individuals and of society as a whole, they will have to try and accept their own homosexuality through the acceptance of those in whom homosexuality is explicit. . . . Why shouldn't everyone be delighted that homosexuals have been entrusted *de facto* with the task and mission of attending the flame, or rather the two original flames, which, if they were to go out, would no longer serve as catalyzers of heterosexuality, thereby bringing about the downfall of the entire system.[9]

Eugene Kennedy points to the same creative role of the homosexual in relationship to the heterosexual community when he writes:

> When men can face with less fear the complex of feelings and impulses that are part of each person's sexuality, they will be able to accept and integrate their experience into a less prejudiced and more creative self-identity. That is to say, when persons can be more friendly toward what really goes on inside them, they will feel less pressure to deny or distort their experience of themselves; the achievement of their masculine or feminine identity will be less the acceptance of a rigidly imposed social stereotype and more the attainment of a multi-dimensioned truth about themselves. Greater openness to self can only increase our chance of more successful gender identity.[10]

Homosexuality and the Relation of the Sexes

In this respect it is interesting to note Jung's appreciation of the positive aspects of the male homosexual condition:

> If we take the concept of homosexuality out of its narrow psychopathological setting and give it a wider connotation, we can see that it has positive aspects as well. . . . This [homosexuality] gives him a great capacity for friendship, which often creates ties of astonishing tenderness between men, and may even rescue friendship between the sexes from its limbo of the impossible. He may have good taste and an aesthetic sense which are fostered by the presence of a feminine streak. Then, he may be supremely gifted as a teacher because of his almost feminine insight and tact. He is likely to have a feeling for history, and to be conservative in the best sense and cherish the values of the past. Often he is endowed with a wealth of religious feelings, which

help him to bring the *ecclesia spiritualis* into reality, and a spiritual receptivity which makes him responsive to revelation.[11]

In the first positive aspect that Jung indicates, he gives us a hint of another function which the homosexual community can play in society at large, one closely allied to the function just treated. Traditionally the married relationship between male and female found its support and stability in social roles, customs, and laws which rendered relatively secondary the type of direct personal relationship between the parties involved. But all these social supports are fast fading away, with the result that, as we have already observed, the divorce rate in the United States has been reported to be rapidly approaching the fifty-percent mark. It is necessary, then, that the human family should find its primary support in the possibility of genuine personal love uniting husband and wife. It is interesting to note that one priest, acting as a canon lawyer in a marriage tribunal, claims that over one-third of the divorce cases he handled were based in the fact that one or the other partner was homosexually inclined. For as I have pointed out, many homosexuals attempt to hide their condition by entering into marriage.

If the homosexual community were allowed to play its role in society with full acceptance, homosexuals would cease to play their present negative role of undermining the marriage relationship, into which they have been forced by their desire to escape detection. Instead, they could potentially be a help in leading society to a new and better understanding of interpersonal love between equals— rather than the role-playing of tradition—as the foundation of the marriage relationship. The source of this liberating function of the homosexual community can be found in Jung's observation that "this [homosexuality] gives him a great capacity for friendship, which often creates ties of astonishing tenderness between men, and may even rescue friendship between the sexes from its limbo of the impossible." As we have seen, one often hears the opinion that homosexuality represents an immature form of sexual development at a narcissistic stage, which prevents the individual from appreciating the difference of the opposite sex. However, if Jung is correct in his observation, frequently it is the male heterosexual who, being under the influence of present sexual-identity images, is preoccupied with the opposite sex as "sexual object" to be dominated. Since he sees the other only in the generic context of sex object, he cannot relate to the other as truly other—that is, as person. Whereas the homosexual, to the extent that he or she has been freed from the depersonalizing effect of these images, is perhaps more free to encounter the opposite sex as total in himself or herself and as equal—that is to say, as person. Consequently, the homosexual community is in a special position to contribute to the liberation of the human community from depersonalized sexual relationships, and thus open up a new possibility of true love and friendship between the sexes.

In a particularly prophetic passage Rainer Maria Rilke had this to say about the changing role of the woman:

> We are only just now beginning to look upon the relation of an individual person to a second individual objectively and without prejudice, and our attempts to live such associations have no model before them. . . . The girl and the woman, in their new, their own unfolding, will but in passing be imitators of masculine ways, good and bad, and repeaters of masculine professions. After the uncertainty of such transitions it will become apparent that women were only going through the profusion and the vicissitudes of those (often ridiculous) disguises in order to cleanse their own charac-

teristic nature of the distorting influence of the other sex. ... This humanity of woman, borne its full time in suffering and humiliation, will come to light when she will have stripped off the conventions of mere femininity in the mutations of her outward status ... some day there will be girls and women whose name will no longer signify merely an opposite of the masculine, but something in itself, something that makes one think, not of any complement or limit, but only of life and existence; the feminine human being. ... This advance will ... change the love experience, which is now full of error, will alter it from the ground up, reshape it into a relation that is meant to be of one human being to another, no longer of man to woman. And this more human love (that will fulfill itself, infinitely considerate, and gentle, and kind and clear in binding and releasing) will resemble that which we are preparing with struggle and toil, the love that consists in this, that two solitudes protect and border and salute each other.[12]

It is the presence of the homosexual element in each individual which will help make such an accomplishment possible; and it is the collective presence of the homosexual community which will help provide the stimulus for such a development.

Homosexuality and Violence

Jung's brief development of the positive aspects of homosexuality indicates still another—and, perhaps, even more important—function that the homosexual community could perform within society toward the liberation of all to a more humane existence. Psychologists are fully aware of the deep all-pervasive relation between the male cultural identity image and the proneness to violence in the human community. As Dr. Weinberg observed, it is homophobia

which frequently underlies the male aggressiveness and
fear of passivity. The male image places an enormous stress
on such elements as aggressivity and domination, qualities
which are concretized in the folk heroes of male society—
the soldier, the prizefighter, the football player, etc. The
traditional need for the male member of society to be ready
courageously to undertake violence in defense of his community explains the historical origins of the emphasis on
these qualities. However, the social and cultural conditions
which made these characteristics of the male necessary and
desirable in the past have changed radically, and as a result
they now pose a serious threat to the peace and progress of
human society in general. Since the Kerner Report on
violence in American culture we are well aware that the
proneness to violence is a serious threat to our society.
Unless we can find nonviolent means to resolve both
national and international problems, humanity itself is
seriously threatened. However, as long as the need of
violence is built into our male-identity image there is little
hope of finding such means. Every new generation will
need its war for its young men to have the opportunity to
prove their virility.

Those prophetic few who have chosen nonviolent means
to try to correct injustices in our society have frequently
been the victims of a popular hatred and antipathy which
borders on the hysterical. Anyone who has participated
in a peace demonstration or a civil-rights march knows from
first-hand experience the type of emotional hostility their
acts can provoke from the typical male onlooker. There
is no doubt that many sense in the behavior of pacifists
and conscientious objectors a menace to the male image
itself.

Hitler's Nazi party was well aware of the association of
pacifism with male homosexuality. In 1928 letters were sent
to all German political parties asking for their position on

reform of paragraph 175 of the German criminal code, a sodomy statute. The Nazi reply was as follows:

Munich 14 May, 1928

Community before Individual!

It is not necessary that you and I live, but it is necessary that the German people live. And they can only live if they can fight, for life means fighting, and they can only fight if they maintain their masculinity. They can only maintain their masculinity if they exercise discipline, especially in matters of love. . . . Anyone who even thinks of homosexual love is our enemy. We reject anything that emasculates our people and makes them a plaything for our enemies, for we know that life is a fight, and it is madness to think that men will ever embrace fraternally. Natural history teaches us the opposite. Might makes right. And the stronger will always win over the weak. Let's see that we once again become the stronger.[13]

The homosexual community, once again granted that they were accepted and respected in the human community at large, have, perhaps, a very special and irreplaceable task to play in freeing the male community from this one-sided emphasis on violent characteristics. Because they may have fortuitously escaped the negative influence of the prevailing male identity image, they are potentially free from the psychological need to establish their male identity by means of violence. Jung's point is not that every homosexual presently realizes such a freedom—any more than every heterosexual necessarily succumbs to the depersonalization of heterosexual images. Occasionally homosexuals imitate in an exaggerated way the worst features of heterosexual images, for example the sadist-masochist style of relation. Violence seems on the whole remarkably absent among self-accepting homosexuals, while particularly prevalent among those who have strong homosexual desires they seek to repress. Norman Mailer's book *Why Are We in Vietnam?* "reveals a vision of America as cursed by the complex and hidden relationships between repression, dread of homosexuality and violence."[14] By liberating the heterosexual male to the possibility of recognizing and accepting the homosexual tendencies in himself, a self-accepting homosexual community could make a positive and decisive contribution to bringing violence within control in society.

Homosexuality and Human Service

Another and connected change is occurring in modern society which also tends to place the person who is living out the traditional male image at a disadvantage. Traditionally the male had to be programmed to be the worker. Rendered insensitive to the needs of persons, he had to find his role in the hard work of dealing with material things. However, the cybernetic revolution has progressively eliminated the amount of hard work with material things necessary for the survival and prosperity of the community. In its place there is a growing demand for more and more people who are able to commit themselves to the types of service to their fellow humans which demand greater sensitivity and human concern. Traditionally, however, the service roles in the community—such as the care of the young and the aged, education, nursing, and social work in general—have been seen as primarily feminine roles, not fit occupations for the true male. As Jung observed, frequently the homosexual is "surprisingly gifted as a teacher because of his almost feminine insight and tact." Thielicke, in turn, speaks of the homosexual as frequently gifted with a remarkable "pedagogical eros, a heightened sense of empathy."[15]

Many observers note the attraction of homosexuals to artistic roles—actors, dancers, decorators, painters, etc.

There is no doubt that the homosexual man is freer to develop aesthetic values than is his male counterpart in the heterosexual world, and thus he has an important role to play in guiding humanity to a deeper appreciation of aesthetic values. However, what has remained relatively unnoticed is the attraction of many homosexuals to service roles, where they have been particularly successful. Many homosexuals find particular satisfaction in such positions as teachers, social workers, hospital orderlies, student counselors, psychologists, clergymen—in fact, in any form of occupation where they can be of direct service to their fellow humans. Three of the most gifted homosexuals for whom it has been my privilege to act as counselor were all extraordinarily successful in their work with retarded children. How often, too, have elderly sick parents been supported and cared for selflessly by a bachelor son or daughter whose homosexuality was carefully hidden from them; whereas, if they had been left to the mercy of their married, heterosexual offspring, they would have been committed to the impersonal care of some institution. Once again, there is the hopeful possibility that the homosexual community could serve the human community as a whole by making the male free to do works of service in the human community without feeling guilty about betraying the standards of his male identity.

Another positive effect that homosexuality can have on individuals, according to Jung, is their "feeling for history" and their resultant tendency "to be conservative in the best sense and cherish the values of the past." Since the majority of the traditional values have their basis in the family structure as such, at first glance this observation of Jung's seems rather paradoxical: for the homosexual appears to many as a threat to the family structure and, as a consequence, a threat to all the values traditionally associated with it. However, most of these traditional values represent customs, mores, and taboos imposed from without to which the majority grant uncritical conformity. Forced because of their condition to live for the most part outside these structures, self-accepting homosexuals are thrown back on themselves and their own experience in order to reestablish the values which merit their acceptance. Almost in direct proportion to the extent that they are cut off from traditional patterns, they must seek out and re-create the real values which these patterns were meant to convey and preserve them by their personal commitment.

Once again, the cultural male-identity image carries with it the frontier spirit of deserting the old in order to construct the new *ab ovo*; whereas the female image carries with it the task of preserving continuity and bringing the best of the old into the new. Homosexuals, by escaping the confines of the male image, are relatively free to develop a sensitivity to the true values of the past, and their isolation from normal structures force them to attempt new incarnations of these values.

The Role of the Lesbian

Unfortunately, Jung's comments were limited for the most part to the positive role of the male homosexual. Let us consider for a moment the specific contribution of the lesbian. Just as the heterosexual male is expected to suppress many human qualities in order to conform to a narrow cultural identity image, even more so the heterosexual female must suppress many essential human qualities—qualities such as spontaneity, aggressiveness, intelligence, initiative, etc.—in order to conform to the narrow cultural identity image of a woman. On occasion the lesbian, by being able to escape the heterosexual cultural identity image, is freer to develop her total personality. In his article "Far from Illness: Homosexuals May Be Healthier than Straights," Dr. Mark Freedman concluded from a series of tests administered to both male homosexuals and to lesbians that "a clear picture of homosexuals today would show a great many men and women who live by their own values and whose emotional expressions aren't limited by traditional sex roles." Many gay people respond to social pressure against homosexuality with an intense quest for identity, purpose, and meaning. Dr. Freedman found the homosexuals he tested superior to their heterosexual counterparts in such psychological qualities as autonomy, spontaneity, orientation toward the present, and increased sensitivity to the value of the person.[16]

Many lesbians feel that they are persecuted by society primarily not because they are lesbians but because they are women. Whereas just the opposite is true for male homosexuals; they are persecuted because they are homosexuals, and not because they are male. Consequently, many lesbians believe that the primary liberation movement to which lesbians should be committed at this point in history is women's liberation, and only secondarily to gay liberation. As we have seen, G. Rattray Taylor, in his book *Sex in History,* finds a universal phenomenon in patriarchal cultures: these cultures always tend to combine a strongly subordinating view of women with a repression and horror of male homosexuality. Whereas cultures based on a matriarchal principle are inclined to combine an enhancement of the status of women with a relative tolerance for male homosexual practices.[17] Consequently, there is an intimate connection between gay liberation for men and women's liberation, so that any real advance in either cause necessarily will represent an advance in the other.

The Homosexual and the Church

These reflections bring us to Jung's final, surprising observation concerning the positive aspects of male homosexu-

ality. This has to do with the particular gift the homosexual
community has received which renders it capable of contributing in a special way to the spiritual development of
humanity.

> He [the homosexual] is endowed with a wealth of reli-
> gious feelings which help him to bring the *ecclesia spi-*
> *ritualis* into reality, and a spiritual receptivity which
> makes him responsive to revelation.[18]

The components of that particular gift have already been
recognized. For we have already noted that the homosexual
community enjoys a special freedom which potentially
could allow it to escape a hyperactive, aggressive, closed
attitude and allow it to be passive and receptive; attitudes
which are essential to prayer and the reception of revelation. It is no accident that in those cultures where the
"macho" image reigns, religious prayer and worship are
considered activities only fit for women. The homosexual
male can be free from a need of violence and dedicated to
the quest of peace. He can have a special sensitivity to the
value of the person, especially the persons of the opposite
sex. He can dedicate himself to a life of service of his fellow
humans. Further, we have seen that the homosexual community, if it were granted freedom to be itself and exercise
its talents, could contribute to the liberation of all humanity
to a fuller realization of personhood.

There is an ideal identity image of what it means to be a
full human person proffered to us by God in the New
Testament; that image is given us in the person of Jesus
Christ. Each of the special qualities Jung attributes to the
homosexual community is usually considered a striking
characteristic of Christ—the qualities which distinguished
him from the ordinary man. Christ had an extraordinary
ability to meet the individual as a unique person; where

others saw a class, a type, a sexual inferior, Christ manifested the ability to encounter the person with understanding and love. He also frequently expressed the desire to
free his disciples from stereotypes and cultural prejudices.
Christ refused to establish his identity and accomplish his
mission by means of violence, and called on his disciples to
be men of peace, resisting injustice by their own suffering.
Again, Christ presented himself as a loving servant of all
humanity, pointing out to his disciples that the pagan seeks
to dominate and to be served, but his disciples must seek
not to be served but to serve.

The point I am trying to make here is, obviously, not that
Christ was a homosexual—any more than he was a heterosexual in the usual significance that the cultural context
gives that designation—but, rather, that he was an extraordinarily full human person and an extraordinarily free
human being. It is interesting to note that many successful
celibate priests and religious, since they have escaped by
means of their celibacy the negative effects of cultural
identity images, have succeeded in incarnating these positive qualities of the Christ image in a striking way.

Paul makes the claim that there was a seed planted by
Christ, the seed of the Spirit, whose eventual fruit will be
the overcoming of all divisions that separate human beings
from one another, and thus separate each of us from the
totality of ourselves (Gal. 3:28). He mentions three such
divisions: master-slave (i.e., all divisions based on aggression and domination), Jew-Greek (i.e., all divisions based
on racial or cultural difference), and finally the division
between male and female. Obviously, Paul is not referring
to an elimination of the biological and—if any—the psychological differences, but to the learned cultural distinction
which renders women inferior to men, denies them the full
status of persons, and thus prevents a true interpersonal
love encounter between men and women. It is this same

cultural distinction which, as we have seen, lies at the base of cultural homophobia and leads to the active persecution of the homosexual.

In Paul's mind, ideal human nature lies in the future, not in the past. It is up to the creative freedom of men and women with God's grace and the model presented in Christ to direct their development toward that ideal. That ideal is the fully mature human person. As I have suggested, the homosexual community, if it is allowed to be itself and develop its special qualities, has a very special role to play in bringing about that ideal both for its own members and for their heterosexual brothers and sisters—until we all "reach mature manhood, and that full measure of development found in Christ" (Eph. 4:13).

This summation of the potentially positive characteristics of the homosexual community runs the danger of creating another stereotype, albeit a positive one. Jung can be misread as portraying a romantic image of homosexuals which suggests that somehow they are better than their heterosexual brothers or sisters. Perhaps the greatest source of prejudice in the past has been the existence of certain negative stereotypes in the popular imagination. The male homosexual was assumed to be effeminate, artistically inclined, cowardly, unfaithful, promiscuous, a hater of women, a child-molester, an active perverter of youth, etc. Lesbians were perceived as violent, aggressive, unfeeling, etc. No more important fact needs to be established than the fact that homosexuals are usually no less varied than their heterosexual counterpart, for the most part no better and no worse. There are violent homosexuals as well as nonviolent; there are artistically sensitive and insensitive, there are relatively selfish and unselfish, religiously sensitive and insensitive, morally committed and uncommitted, weak and strong, sexually promiscuous and faithful. Consequently, I have no desire to create a new stereotype, albeit a positive one.

The true fact is that there is no such being as a homosexual, any more than there is such a being as a heterosexual: there are human beings who happen to be, relatively, heterosexually or homosexually inclined. And these persons are as varied in their qualities and sensitivities as is humanly possible. Consequently, to assume that any general characteristic, whether negative or positive, necessarily applies in each particular case leads to a falsification of reality. Rather, we must be prepared to meet each individual person, whether heterosexually or homosexually inclined, on his or her own merits without the falsification of the encounter that comes from stereotypes. Charles Curran has remarked that "homosexuality can never be an ideal." I agree completely. But then, heterosexuality as such can never be an ideal either. The only ideals involved in all questions of sexual orientation are the great transcendent questions of justice and love.

The essential point I have tried to establish in stressing the positive characteristics of homosexuality is that the tendency to identify oneself as a person with one's sexual-identity image can, and frequently does, lead to a one-sided stress on certain qualities and the elimination of others. Heterosexuals tend to define themselves in contrast to homosexuals; homosexuals, in turn, tend to define themselves in contrast to heterosexuals. The result is a narrow, impoverished, and dehumanizing self-image for both parties. The objective acceptance of the homosexual community will potentially leave both communities free from the need to conform to narrow stereotypes, and positively free to develop all the qualities that belong to the fullness of the human personality.

Part 3

Pastoral Ministry to the Homosexual Community

The Failure of Pastoral Ministry

One final problem from the viewpoint of moral theology remains to be explored; that is the necessary changes in the nature of the Church's ministry to the homosexual community, granting the change in the nature of the Church's moral judgment on homosexual relationships which I have argued for. Paul Lehmann, as we have seen, made the point that the concern of Christian ethics should be to relate the intimate reality of sex in all its forms, including homosexuality, to the freedom and integrity of human wholeness. Consequently, Christian sexual ethics should accent the fundamental importance of the sexual act for the humanization of men and women and the setting in which that humanization is a concrete and achievable reality.[1] How, then, from the Church's viewpoint can it provide the spiritual setting within which the homosexual community can achieve its fullest moral and spiritual development?

There is no question that in the past the Church has made no attempt in this direction. It will be recalled that in its resolution on ministry to the homosexual community in

153

Denver in 1972, the National Federation of Priests' Councils
reported that "the Church's concern for and ministry to the
homosexual community is practically invisible and therefore
non-existent in the United States." Consequently, the Federation voted to establish "a task force to develop a model for
a Christian ministry to the homosexual community."[2]

The nonexistence of such a ministry in the past is easily
understood. Since it regarded the homosexual condition
and all homosexual relationships at best as necessarily
"objectively sinful" and somehow contrary to the divine
will, the Church logically has refused to grant any recognition to homosexual relationships and, thus, to the homosexual community as such. Individual priest-counselors and
confessors have manifested genuine compassion and pastoral concern for the individual penitent. It should be remarked, however, that the priest, like the psychiatrist,
tended to encounter only those homosexuals who have
internalized the judgment of the Church and of society, and
hence experienced their condition as somehow sinful and
productive of guilt and self-contempt. And frequently, since
the priest has himself shared society's homophobia, even
that minimal human compassion for the penitent has been
lacking. A number of years ago a report by a Lutheran pastor
on a West Coast conference on homosexuality carried the
following headlines in a Catholic newspaper: "Homosexuals Ask Churches to Accept Them." In that report one
of the homosexuals interviewed at the conference had this
to say:

The Church is only for the majority and is always mea-
suring up to conformity. I have no place to go, and it's
impossible to become an atheist. First of all, every guy
has got to have some place to go, even if he is not a
devout and saintly person. Going to Church and con-
fession sort of makes a person feel that he isn't alone.

After all, a bed partner is only for a couple of minutes, hours or for a whole night—but God lasts forever. If the Church would only recognize that we are all members of the flock. They don't have to bless homosexuality or say it's fine, but just say: You are a little spotted, but you are children of the flock.

Not only homosexuals themselves but many professional people who deal with homosexuals believe that very frequently the Church tends to reject the homosexual. In the introduction to his book *Toward a Christian Understanding of the Homosexual*, H. Kimball-Jones, a Methodist minister and counselor whom I have quoted earlier, has this to say:

There are untold thousands of homosexuals in America today who are forced to live secret lives, forced to live in constant doubt and fear, lest they be discovered and labeled as outcasts of society. . . . Their sexual anomaly has made them potential criminals in the eyes of the law and sinners in the eyes of the Church. The Church for the most part has made no attempt to understand them; along with the rest of society, it has viewed them with great contempt, closing its doors to them, failing to recognize them as children of God.[3]

In their book *Counseling the Catholic*, Robert Gleason and George Hagmaier make the point that many homosexuals feel abandoned by the Church because of inept pastoral counseling:

The tragic reception which many a homosexual has received from a well-meaning but ineffectual or sometimes even hostile priest at least partially explains how so many of these unfortunates leave the Church in frustrated rebellion or deep despair . . . it is easy for him to conclude that the Church has abandoned him too.[4]

Gordon Westwood, in his work *A Minority: A Report on the Life of the Male Homosexual in Great Britain*, noted that 61 percent of his homosexual contacts had turned at one time to the Church for help, but only 6 percent said that they obtained help with their homosexual problem from their religion; while 5 percent more stated that their religious belief had offered them some comfort. However, 81 percent reported no help or comfort from religion.[5] As John Cavanaugh pointed out in a lecture at Catholic University:

> Many counselors look upon the homosexual with mixed feelings. They have been known to be fearful, mistrusting, resentful, and sometimes overcome by feelings of inadequacy. Many have frightened the deviate away with their rudeness and hostility. They may associate all homosexuality with willful depravity, seduction of the young, effeminacy, and moral perversion. . . . Because of these attitudes many homosexuals do not seek advice, which may lead some counselors to think that homosexuality is a rare thing. I have been told by priests of over twenty years experience that they have never seen a homosexual.[6]

Personal Ministry to the Individual

Most experts are in agreement that members of the clergy, granted that they have minimal knowledge of the psychological aspects of homosexuality and are free from popular prejudices and misconceptions, can be of important and even essential help to the homosexual, and especially to a member of their Church who has this problem and seeks their assistance. More frequently than not, persons with a problem concerning their homosexuality have introjected the attitude of society toward themselves. They suffer great mental anguish and a profound sense of alienation, often believing themselves to be outcasts not only from human society but from divine love as well. No person with heterosexual tendencies would be inclined to answer the question, Who are you? with the response: I am a heterosexual. But if they felt free to do so, this would be the response of homosexuals. Whether they carefully conceal their homosexual condition or express it openly, people with a homosexual orientation tend to accept their homosexuality as their deepest self-identity image, the most important single fact about themselves. And because they tend to accept their image from the attitudes of the people about them, persons who believe themselves to be homosexual frequently have a negative self-image which leads to self-hatred and self-destruction.

Homosexuals will never be able to master their sexual drive in a positive way and integrate it successfully into their whole personality development until they become aware of themselves as persons of infinite dignity and worth, worthy of their fellow human's respect and consideration. In order to eliminate a self-destructive image and arrive at a positive self-identity image of themselves as persons of value, it is absolutely necessary that persons who have a homosexual orientation find someone with whom they can be completely open and still be treated with respect and love. What militates against such a self-disclosure, however, is the frequent conviction that no one will continue to respect them as persons if they reveal the true nature of their sexuality.

Logically, by their calling and profession, clergy should be the persons to whom the homosexual could turn with complete confidence. And very often—some authors estimate at least forty percent of the time—the member of the clergy is the first person to whom homosexuals turn for help. If, however, the homosexual should fail to receive a sympathetic reception, which unfortunately often seems to be the case, he or she could easily lose all hope. On the other hand, the very fact of being able to speak openly about their sexuality for the first time with a respected member of the community, who continues to manifest respect for them, can be an essential step toward establishing hope, where previously there was only despair.

Even when the rare clergypersons who understand the homosexual and have the courage to offer ministry can be found, the very fact that they do such counseling can effectively ruin their career and destroy their reputation as clergy. The National Federation of Priests' Councils notes that "individual priests and ministers, working with homosexuals, usually encounter a social and psychological stigma as a result of their work, and this stigma is the single most effective obstacle to ministers who want to work with homosexuals."

The Church and the Reform of Civil Law

There is no question that frequently homosexuals in the United States today are the victims of great social injustice. They are frequently denied the fundamental human rights to association, work, housing, etc. The first step toward eliminating these injustices is a reform of law. We have seen how a legal tradition of suppression of homosexual practices sprang up in the Christian West as a result of a misunderstanding of the Sodom and Gomorrah narrative. In a hearing concerning the reform of legal discrimination against homosexuals in employment and housing in New York City, one politician found it necessary to oppose the bill because it would be contrary to "our Judaic-Christian heritage." He attempted to establish this point by referring to the Sodom and Gomorrah tradition. The Church obviously has a serious obligation to correct such a misunderstanding of authentic Christian tradition in the minds of the public.

Practically all the authorities consulted are in agreement that there is an urgent need from a legal viewpoint for reform of the present laws in the United States concerning homosexuality. Such reforms have been operative in most European countries since the Napoleonic Code, without any evident harm to the common good. Great Britain adopted these reforms in 1967 as a result of the Wolfenden Commission Report. In a majority of states in the United States homosexual acts between consenting adults are legally a criminal act, penalized in some states with long prison terms.

At the time of the Wolfenden Report debate in England, the Catholic Archbishop of Westminster acknowledged two "questions of fact" which, he believed, should determine the question of law reform. "Catholics," he commented, "are free to make up their minds on these two questions of fact." The two questions were:

1. If the law takes cognizance of private acts of homosexuals and makes them crimes, do worse evils follow for the common good?
2. Would change in the law harm the common good by seeming to condone homosexual conduct?

All authorities seem to agree in answering "yes" to the first question. There is little doubt that the present repressive laws against homosexuals quite unjustly penalize a minority group and cause unnecessary and untold pain, fear, and suffering to many people who are otherwise law-abiding and responsible citizens. Apart from the fearful toll of suffering, lost talent, and mental breakdown, etc., the present laws considerably increase criminal activity by the opportunity they offer for blackmail, entrapment, and other forms of intimidation. A trial in New York uncovered a blackmail ring that had earned millions of dollars in this manner.

The type of abuse these laws lead to on the political level is notorious. By giving the homosexual community the character of an outlawed minority these laws encourage a type of aggression based in homophobia. On many occasions the illegal status of the homosexual has combined with an emotional climate to give rise to hostility approaching psychotic proportions and violence that is unequivocally criminal. Once exposed or even suspected, the "homosexual" may become prey to the worst forms of cruelty and injustice at the hands of those who regard their cruelty as righteousness. On numerous occasions individuals or groups of men have established themselves "vigilantes" and have undertaken the practice of "queer baiting." One example, an instance which ended in tragedy for all concerned, occurred in San Francisco. A group of young men (two of them from a private Catholic school) attacked, robbed, and assaulted a young school teacher they judged to be "queer." They left him unconscious on the street, where he was killed by an oncoming trolley—while the vigilantes continued their prowl of the city, looking for other victims. The inspector assigned to the case reported: "They said they considered Hall's death a justifiable homicide. They seem to regard the beating of whoever they consider deviants as a civic duty."

The moral question here concerns the source of the impression these young men had that assault and battery, robbery, and even murder are justified if the object of one's hostility is homosexual, or even only suspected to be so. Certainly even the clergyperson who feels most strongly about the evils of homosexual practices has a duty in conscience to refrain from any words or actions which would help create the atmosphere in which such events become likely, or from seeming to give tacit approval.

The American Law Institute in its model penal code recommended as far back as 1955 that private homosexual acts between consenting adults should be excluded from the criminal law because

> no harm to the secular interest of the community is involved, and there is a fundamental question of the protection to which every individual is entitled against State interference in his personal affairs when he is not hurting others.

The second question of fact the archbishop asks is much more difficult to answer. It is, perhaps, true that many people believe what is legal is moral and what is immoral should be illegal. This popular confusion between legality and morality is the most serious obstacle to law reform. We have seen this confusion at work in the minds of many, for example, in the question of the reform of laws concerning abortion. The experience in the past with prohibition and in other fields has led the public to some realization that "one should not try to legislate morality." The emphasis in the Catholic Church since Vatican II on the right and responsibility of the individual to come to an independent moral judgment has also helped pave the way.

However, Christian educators and clergy cannot be content with merely registering a question of fact here. In the whole field of sexual morality there is a widespread confusion of morality with legality, to the serious detriment of the moral life. Most confessors and counselors are well aware how often the marriage license, for example, is understood as a license for an immoral use and abuse of one's marriage partner. Consequently, a serious responsibility rests on the shoulders of all who are involved in helping to form the conscience of the public to provide instruction in the ability to distinguish and to relate the moral and legal orders with their respective ends and procedures. This would prepare the way for a reform of law as well as a more mature attitude toward personal moral responsibility.

Some traditional authors express alarm that any let-up of legal discipline might result in a marked increase in homosexual behavior. But first of all, such legal reforms will certainly not contribute to any increase in the homosexual condition. There is no evidence that the legal status of homosexuality in any way influences the number of those who share this condition. However, there is a good reason to believe that the healthier climate that would result from such a legal reform could reduce the social pressures and consequent emotional disorders for those who share this condition. Second, there is no evidence that homosexual practices have increased in those societies where no such legal penalties exist or where they have recently been reformed. All these considerations lead to the conclusion that the Church has a serious moral responsibility out of both justice and charity to work for the reform of laws concerning homosexuals and do everything in its power to educate the faithful to the need of such a reform.

The Goal of Heterosexual Adjustment

[Author's note: I have changed my opinion on this matter. For my current thinking, see appendix 1, p. 201.] Once he or she has established a positive relationship of understanding and respect, the clergy counselor's difficult task has just begun. If the clergyperson is to offer the homosexual anything more than the essential step of acceptance in Christ, he or she must have some understanding of the nature of the individual's problem. Practically all authorities agree that the first goal of counseling should be to guide the person with a homosexual problem to a heterosexual adjustment whenever possible.

The person who merely fears he or she may be a homosexual, or is attracted to the homosexual community, should explore every avenue toward the achievement of normal heterosexual capacities and relationships. This direction should be taken independent of what one's moral judgment may be concerning homosexual practices. Even the officers of the Mattachine Society, a homophile organization, agree with this aim:

> On the basis of our experience—the embarrassment, shame and humiliation so many of us have known—we would definitely advise anyone who has not yet become an active homosexual, but has only misgivings about himself, to go the other way, if he can.

The reason for this advice is the many problems average homosexuals encounter, which make a positive adjustment to such a life extremely difficult. Among these difficulties can be enumerated: the agonies of remorse and self-torture over what typical homosexuals feel to be their immoral desires, whether these arise from conscious identity with the condemnations of Church and society or from neurotic conflicts within themselves; their openness to blackmail and other forms of intimidation; their status of being outside the normal protection of the law; their necessity continually to conceal what they frequently believe to be their true identity from public view, with the added threat that accidental revelation could result in loss of their job, expulsion from school, dishonorable discharge from the military service, loss of future security and job opportunities, loss of friends and the respect of family and dependents. Still other problems involve their propensity to sexual promiscuity divorced from a complete and healthy interpersonal relationship; and the resulting tendency for sexual desires indulged in, but never fully satisfied, to occupy a disproportionate place in their life. Above all else, there is the very real threat of ultimate loneliness to one to whom all the normal structures of society—marriage, children, dependents, etc.—are closed. It should be noted, however, that all these negative aspects of homosexuality are not due to homosexuality as such, but are the results of both society's and the Church's attitude to the homosexual.

All these rather common aspects of homosexual life can effectively paralyze all initiative, result in a feeling of inferiority, and lead to an emotional breakdown which could make social adjustment impossible. Therefore, if there is any hope of heterosexual adjustment, that escape from the difficulties of homosexual life should be explored.

So, the first discernment a counselor should attempt to establish is whether or not a given individual is a genuine homosexual or merely suffering from "pseudo-homosexual panic" as a result of some experience of one of the many forms of conditional homosexuality. This discernment is especially important, as Hettlinger notes, in dealing with the adolescent or young adult. Quoting experts to the effect that "it is not until the age of twenty-five has been reached or even later that we can be fairly sure that homosexual impulses are not just a phase of normal development," Hettlinger concludes:

> Even if on examination a student has markedly homosexual tendencies, no one within the normal student age range has reason to conclude that his homosexual urges, however strong, are either basic or permanent.[7]

D. J. West concurs in this judgment, stating: "When homosexual behavior represents a precarious solution to current conflicts or reflects the pressures of external circumstances, a change may well come about."[8] In such cases it is sometimes sufficient to point out the negative side of homosexual life and its obvious disadvantages in order to cure any illusions of homosexuality or any false images of a "gay" life. I know of one situation where a student-counselor was able to use the help of an older, well-adjusted homosexual to achieve this purpose with excellent results.

Whenever possible, of course, clergy-counselors are well advised to seek professional assistance in dealing with homosexuals. Where such assistance can be had, most authors agree that clergy themselves should continue to see the individual and seek to offer supportive guidance in cooperation with the professional involved. In cases where the individual refuses such help, or for practical reasons such help is unavailable, the clergy themselves should continue their role as counselor and do the best they can. In this latter event, the clergy should themselves seek supervision in the management of their client.

Several moral problems face the counselor who accepts as the primary goal to lead the homosexual to a heterosexual adjustment. Among these is the problem of the danger of fostering false hopes of a change in sexual orientation in the mind of the homosexual. Despite the optimism of some psychiatrists concerning the possibilities of change, there is little real hope that change will be effected in the practical order for a large majority of the cases of true homosexuality. Even Bieber, one of the most optimistic psychiatrists, reports that only twenty-seven percent of his patients changed their orientation under optimum conditions. As Cory and LeRoy remark in their book *The Homosexual and His Society*:

Of those who came (or were sent) to Bieber and his co-workers for study, who struggled through analysis and underwent the torment and difficulties that it entails, many of them for literally hundreds of hours, more than 70 percent remained homosexuals. The writers are acquainted with hundreds of young men and women, and many older ones as well, who spent thousands of hard-earned dollars and hundreds of uncomfortable hours, seeking to overcome their imperious deviant drives, but in vain. The Mattachine Society and other groups have scores of members, some of whom readily admit that they were aided to face reality by the therapeutic sessions, but who were as overwhelmingly or as exclusively homosexual after therapy as they had been before.

It would seem that 73 percent of failure is a large figure, and that this is the realistic statistic that should be publicized in order to obtain better self-understanding by the homosexual and better acceptance of him by society. To focus attention on the 27 percent, as if it were a sure-fire majority, is misleading and dangerous.[9]

As a consequence the counselor would be well advised to admit the limited chances of a therapeutic change in more serious cases where the conditions are unfavorable. As William Lynch established in his book *Images of Hope*, nothing can be more destructive psychologically than to hold out a false hope to an already disturbed person. The counselor should also emphasize, however, that regardless of the question of heterosexual adaptation, therapy can still be of great benefit. Well over ninety percent of Bieber's patients reported "improvement which was not directly related to the sex problem." There is no doubt, then, that therapy can be very helpful to anyone suffering psychologically because of a homosexual problem, while in a limited number of cases it can result in a heterosexual adjustment. As we have seen, connected with the issue of false hope is the danger of false guilt, if analysis fails to change sexual orientation. As I have already pointed out, the great stress some clinicians place on the a priori condition on the part of the patient of a will to change as a necessary factor for the success of analysis could lead many into further depths of self-accusation and despair. For if therapy should fail, they could easily draw the false conclusion that the failure of therapy was due to a failure of their will, for which they are morally responsible.

The Case For and the Case Against Sexual Abstinence

[Author's note: I have changed my opinion on this matter. For my current thinking, see appendix 1, pp. 201]. There is another factor that seriously hampers the ability of the Church to minister effectively to the homosexual. Granted the traditional moral judgment that homosexual relations are always necessarily sinful and contrary to the divine will, the only pastoral advice that could be given to the true homosexual, who could not change his or her sexual orientation, was to practice sexual abstinence. In the words of Michael Buckley:

> The aim of all pastoral counseling of the homosexual should be ultimately his re-orientation to heterosexuality, and where this is impossible an adjustment to his condition in the only way acceptable to Catholic moral theology—a life of chastity.[10]

Cavanaugh agrees with Buckley, stating: "A clergyman should be content to set as his ultimate aim the adjustment of the homosexual to a life of chastity."[11] It is clear from the context of both authors that they understand by "chastity" uniquely a policy of total abstinence from all sexual expression. Neither author seems aware that there can be a chaste expression of sexuality insofar as it is a true expression of human love.

All moral considerations apart for the moment, there is no question that a life of abstinence from all sexual expression, if that life proves possible without serious damage to the person, remains a good prudential choice for the homosexual in today's society. The dangers and the difficulties of an active homosexual life are so great and the probability that, owing to guilt and self-hatred, a homosexual relationship may prove destructive both to the individual and to the other person involved is so high, that every Christian homosexual may be well advised to try to structure his life without an active sexual relationship. As a result, if there is any hope that a life of abstinence can be successfully undertaken, then it remains a reasonable choice. It should be noted once again, however, that all these negative aspects of homosexuality are not necessarily due to homosexuality as such but are the result of both society's and the Church's attitude to the homosexual.

Clergy counselors should show a sensitive awareness of what they in fact are demanding of a homosexual when they urge him or her to undertake such a life of abstinence. For example, Cavanaugh's statement: "Just as we expect the heterosexual to be continent outside of marriage, so, too, the homosexual"[12] demonstrates just such a lack of sensitivity to the homosexual's special dilemma. The heterosexual's abstinence is either a temporary condition or one that has been freely chosen; whereas the abstinence the Church would impose on the homosexual is involuntary and unending. In attempting to live out a life of abstinence, the adult homosexual will first of all have to avoid any close relationship with the opposite sex. Such a friendship in our culture would almost certainly be understood as a prelude to marriage. And if there is any advice one can almost certainly give in most cases, it is that the homosexual is morally obligated never to enter marriage while there is any reasonable doubt that he or she may be a true homosexual. In fact, canon lawyers are seriously debating the question whether or not such a marriage would be necessarily invalid, since a true homosexual would be incapable of a valid consent to the marriage bond. There are many instances reported where homosexuals have entered into marriage, concealing their condition from their partner, in order to disguise their condition and win social acceptance. The tragic results for all parties concerned need not be detailed.

Cut off from close relations with the opposite sex because of his or her condition, the homosexual is traditionally exhorted to cut off any deep, personal relationships with persons of the same sex because they would serve as "the occasion of sin." Cavanaugh advises the counselor to urge the male homosexual to avoid all former homosexual companions; in forming new friendships, to avoid any individual who is "sexually attractive"; to live alone; to avoid work with boys; to avoid entry into the military service; not to enter the clergy or religious life, etc. Indeed, he carries this type of advice to its logical conclusions by advising that the homosexual should avoid any "romantic" friendships, even if chaste:

> One of the principles of conduct that an invert should formulate is that, because of his special condition, there is no value in allowing himself to form or to continue romantic friendships (i.e., those in which sexual attraction is a determining element) with people of his own sex, no matter how chaste the relation may be. Even if the invert is continent in these friendships, it is, nevertheless, a human love which can be never fully realized or satisfied licitly. It will, therefore, inevitably lead to anxiety and depression.[13]

In other words, in the pursuit of a life of "chastity" homosexuals should deny themselves not only genital sexual relations, but every expression of warm human affection. Every competent therapist is well aware that all human affection and friendship is normally colored by a diffused, nongenital form of sexual attraction. Cut off, then, from all deep and affectionate female and male friendship, the homosexual is condemned to a living hell of isolation and loneliness. And such a life is not urged temporarily, but must be sustained until death, under threat of possible eternal damnation. As black novelist James Baldwin observes:

> The really horrible thing about present-day homosexuality . . . is that today's unlucky deviate can only save himself by the most tremendous exertion of all his forces from falling into an underworld in which he can never meet either man or woman, where it is impossible to have either a lover or a friend, where the possibility of genuine human involvement has altogether ceased. When this possibility has ceased, so has the possibility of growth.[14]

Cavanaugh somewhat tempers his advice, however, by quoting the following from Hagmaier and Gleason:

> The uninformed confessor has a tendency to demand that the invert avoid every contact which might possibly be a source of stimulation for him, e.g., swimming, sports, stag society, artistic circles, male friendships. In many cases such involvements help drain off a more basic urge for physical contact. To stifle these outlets could very well precipitate the penitent into more frequent and more overt homosexual activity.[15]

In line with this advice, those writing from a traditional viewpoint frequently advise homosexuals to sublimate their sexual urges by committing themselves to an active and productive life. What they sometimes fail to realize is that they have eliminated a priori under the rubric of "avoiding the occasion of sin" those very activities for which the homosexual is very often best suited, and by means of which he or she would have some chance of achieving a wholesome sublimination. As Kimball-Jones observes:

> While he might stand the best chance of sublimating his sexual drives in professions such as scouting, teaching and the Christian ministry, professions which involve what Thielicke calls a "pedagogical eros . . . a heightened sense of empathy," it is difficult for a professed homosexual to enter into such professions.[16]

There is a growing body of evidence that for a majority of true homosexuals sublimation and a life of sexual abstinence is not a practical pastoral answer to their problem. Counselors sometimes seem to be unaware of, or forget, the fact that psychologists understand sublimation as an unconscious process, which, as a result, cannot be the direct object of one's will. As Gordon Westwood indicates, "Sublimation is an unconscious mechanism and can be a useful aid, but it is rarely a full controlling factor. Whereas forced abstinence from fear and guilt often leads to neurotic disorders."[17] Ellis and West both report sublimation relatively ineffective as a therapeutic goal.[18] Marcus Hirshfield found such therapy to be effective in less than five percent of the homosexuals with whom he attempted it.[19]

Unfortunately, since the role of permanent confessor or spiritual father has all but disappeared from the scene in the United States, most confessors do not have any sort of follow-up on the penitents they advise. But those clergy-counselors who do stay with the persons they direct are well aware how frequently the true homosexual who attempts a life of abstinence will go a month, a year, even several years, only to end up indulging in promiscuous, often compulsive sex, calculated to lead to social ruin and psychological breakdown. In homosexual circles the person who leads a life of abstinence in his or her home town, only to fall victim to the worse forms of promiscuity with all its inherent dangers on an annual visit to the big city, is a notorious figure.

The insistence of the Church on total abstinence as the only morally feasible alternative for the genuine homosexual who cannot change his or her sexual orientation has led to the paradoxical result, even if unintentional, of promoting promiscuity and humanly destructive and depersonalized sexual activity among Catholic homosexuals. A Catholic homosexual who confessed occasional promiscuity could receive absolution and be allowed to receive communion in good conscience. If, however, that person had entered into a genuine permanent love relationship, he or she would be judged in "a state of sin," and unless the person expressed a willingness to break off that relationship he or she would be denied absolution. Consequently, the traditional discipline unwittingly tended to undermine the development of healthy interpersonal relationships among homosexuals and gave the appearance that the Church disapproved more of the love between homosexuals than it did of their sexual activity as such. One can see a parallel here with the similar paradoxical result of the Church's attitude on fornication and cohabitation. If a Catholic were involved in promiscuous heterosexual activity, he or she could receive absolution. However, individuals who entered into a permanent relationship outside of marriage, and thus attempted to establish a fuller human relationship, were judged to be in "a state of sin" and must be denied absolution and the right to receive holy communion.

Again I restate, if a person with homosexual tendencies with God's grace can successfully undertake a life of abstinence without destructive emotional conflicts and personality breakdown, then he or she is certainly well advised to do so. But what is troubling many counselors and confessors, as well as many moral theologians, is the realization that a majority of their clients or penitents who fall into the category of true homosexuals will in all probability not be successful in such an attempt, no matter how hard they pray or strive. On the contrary, the almost inevitable results will be tragic in terms of suffering, guilt, and mental disorder. The whole enterprise becomes all the more suspect with the dawning awareness that the moral judgment which makes such a pastoral practice necessary is not so much a true moral judgment as it is an expression of historical and cultural prejudice.

There are a number of other factors which are causing many to question the absolute validity of the Church's traditional pastoral stance in relation to the homosexual. Surely, the present crisis concerning a life of abstinence in the priesthood and religious life should give rise to some reconsideration. If priests and religious, who attempt a life of chastity under optimum conditions of both nature and grace, are finding difficulty in ever growing numbers, how can we demand such a life from the average homosexual, who shares none of the helps or motivations to be found in clerical or religious life?

One factor which probably influences the absolute nature of the traditional stand has to do with clerical values and mentality. In an interesting research study into the differences between typical clerical and lay value systems, priest-psychologist William Hague discovered that whereas the priest is inclined to rate "salvation" first in his scale of values, the layperson is inclined to place "love" first and give "salvation" a relatively lower rating. Hague makes this observation:

> We find our identity in our relationships with others.
> One cannot base an identity on mere superficial
> "helping" relationships, no matter how dedicated or
> religious the motives may be. When a crisis comes,
> there isn't the personal human security there to with-
> stand it. . . . Deep intimate human relationships are the
> ground in which personality takes roots and lasting se-
> curity is found.[20]

Hague suggests that this insight helps explain the number
of excellent men—still very much in love with their priesthood—who have chosen to leave it for a more personal
relationship of marriage. In an analogous fashion, many
homosexuals are faced with the dilemma of continuing their
relationship with the Church at the price of their loss of any
deep human relationship and the loss of their own growth
and development in their personal self-identity, or of seeking their personal growth and identity by means of such a
relationship only at the price of cutting themselves off from
the Church. Just as many priests are of the opinion that
celibacy should not be a necessary condition of their
priesthood but open to voluntary choice, so many Catholic
homosexuals believe that a life of sexual abstinence should
not be required of them because of their condition but open
to voluntary choice.

The traditional exhortations that homosexuals can
achieve sanctity by accepting the sufferings and difficulties
which would result from the diminishment of their personal
lives and their psychological problems seem to be based
frequently on a very questionable sort of dualism between
human and spiritual development. They tend to negate the
implications of insight attributed to Saint Irenaeus: "The
glory of God is humans fully alive." One recalls Saint
Augustine's exhortation to one of the first communities of
religious, in which he points out that "the foolish virgins
without oil in their lamps" were indeed chaste, but their

chastity was without love; they were incapable of a warm, loving response to the human needs of others, and thus were excluded from the kingdom of God, which is a kingdom of love. There can be a type of sexual abstinence which tends to be morally evil and psychologically destructive. There can be no necessary conflict between the human and spiritual fulfillment of humanity.[21]

What Kimball-Jones suggests is that if the Church is to be of any help to the majority of true homosexuals who cannot change or successfully lead a life of abstinence, then it must begin at the point where they find themselves. The question is not whether or not they are in a state of sin, but rather how they can make the best of a given, and in many cases, unchangeable situation. As Thielicke poses the question:

> Perhaps the best way to formulate the ethical problem of the constitutional homosexual, who because of his vitality is not able to practice abstinence, is to ask whether in the coordinated system of his constitution, he is willing to structure the man-man relationship in an *ethically responsible* way. Thus the ethical question meets him on the basis which he did not enter intentionally, but which is where he actually finds himself. . . .[22]

Ministry to the Homosexual Community

These and many other factors have led the homosexual community in general and the Christian homosexual community in particular to a new level of consciousness concerning its needs and its rights in relation to the Church. Many Christian homosexuals no longer accept the traditional judgment that all homosexual relationships, precisely because they are homosexual, are necessarily sinful. Consequently, they are refusing the pastoral aim of abstinence as a necessary goal and, in many cases, as a desirable goal. As one group of Catholic homosexuals reported:

The primary purpose of *Dignity* is to help the gay
Catholic realize that to be Christian he need not deny
his homosexuality, but rather he *should* be fully himself in order to be fully Christian. Dignity will fight for
the right of the gay to use sex his own way. We have
no intention of side-stepping the issue, or playing it
down, or steering our members toward a celibate life.
We do not want people merely to accept us as human
beings. We want them to accept the fact that because
we are human we have the right to use sex in the only
way that is natural for us. When that is accepted, we
will be seen very easily as morally and physically
healthy, patriotic human beings.[23]

Further, important as individual counseling has been
and remains, it is no longer possible for the Church to
perceive its ministry to the homosexual as a ministry to
individuals as such; rather, it must begin to recognize that
the only effective ministry will be a ministry to the homosexual community. Christian homosexuals have an imperative need of a social and religious setting in which they can
begin the long task of repairing the wounds inflicted on
their psyches by the prejudices of society and the Church,
as well as the positive task of attempting to integrate moral
and religious values into their life-style as self-accepting
homosexuals. From their sociological study of male homosexuality in three countries—the United States, the Neth-
erlands, and Denmark—Weinberg and Williams concluded: "Probably our most salient finding pertains to the
beneficial effects (in terms of psychological adjustment) of a
supportive environment—social relations with other homosexuals, their own institutions and publications."[24]
Christian homosexuals are well aware that such a religious community can be truly helpful to them only if it is
willing to accept them as homosexual and accept ethically
responsible homosexual relationships. The failure of the

mainline churches to provide the homosexual with such a community has led to the establishment of the "gay" churches, such as the Metropolitan Community Church.[25] These homophile churches conceive of themselves as interim communities, necessary as long as the heterosexual church communities are incapable of receiving, or unwilling to receive, homosexuals while respecting their lifestyle. The Metropolitan Community Church, for example, claims that it is

> working toward the day when it can close its doors because the other Christian communities with love and understanding will have opened theirs to the gay people. Since the founding of the Church, it has occasionally been necessary for someone to step outside the regular Christian camp in order to point out its laxity in adhering to the loving spirit of its founder. . . . Each of these moments of re-evaluation of the Church's mission resulted in advances in mankind's eternal struggle to establish an environment in which every person has the opportunity to fully realize and develop his potential as a human being and a child of God. Metropolitan Community Church is following this great tradition of endeavoring to be God's special instrument in waking up the institutional Church to its lack of responsiveness of the will of God.[26]

In a check on three homophile congregations in the New York City area, I found that a sizable number, perhaps even a majority, of the large groups in attendance at Sunday services were believing Catholics or former Catholics. Most of those interviewed expressed a strong desire to return to the practice of their faith, but only on condition that the Church would be willing to accept them as they are.

Among Catholic homophiles the most important attempt to date to establish such a community—one that accepts homosexuals as they are and yet remains within the Catholic Church community—is that of Dignity, whose newsletter is quoted above. In their original statement of Position and Purpose, the members of Dignity give the following description of themselves:

A. We believe that Gay Catholics are members of Christ's Mystical Body, numbered among the people of God. We have an inherent dignity because God created us, Christ died for us, and the Holy Spirit sanctified us in Baptism, making us his temple, and the channel through which the love of God might become visible. Because of this, it is our right, our privilege and our duty to live the sacramental life of the Church, so that we might become more powerful instruments of God's love working among all people.

B. We believe that Gays can express their sexuality in a manner that is consonant with Christ's teaching. We believe that all sexuality should be exercised in an ethically responsible and unselfish way.

C. As members of DIGNITY we wish to promote the cause of the Gay community. To do this, we must accept our responsibility to the Church, to Society and to individual Gay Catholics:

1. To the Church: to work for the development of its sexual theology and for the acceptance of Gays as full and equal members of Christ.
2. To Society: to work for justice and social acceptance through education and legal reform.
3. To individual Gays: to reinforce their self-acceptance and their sense of dignity, and to aid them in becoming more active members of Church and Society.

D. Dignity is organized to unite all Gay Catholics, to develop leadership and to be an instrument through which the Gay Catholic may be heard by the Church and Society. There are four areas of concern:

1. Spiritual Development: We shall strive to achieve Christian maturity through all the means at our disposal, especially the Mass, the sacraments, personal prayer and active love of the neighbor.
2. Education: We wish to inform ourselves in all matters of faith as well as in all that concerns the Gay community so that we may develop the maturity of outlook needed to live fulfilling lives in which sexuality and spirituality are integrated, and to prepare us for service in the Gay community.
3. Social Involvement: As Catholics and as members of Society we shall become involved in those actions that bring the love of Christ to others and provide the basis for social reform.
   a. Toward individuals: We wish to live a life of service to others, hoping to render visible the love of Christ and contributing our share to building a community of love.
   b. With Gay groups: We wish to work with other Gay groups for the cause of justice to the Gay community and for the promotion of a sense of solidarity.
   c. With religious and secular groups: We wish to work with them that they may better understand Gays and recognize present injustices.
4. Social Events: Activities of a social and recreational nature will be provided to promote an atmosphere where friendships can develop and mature, and where the Gay's sense of acceptance and dignity may be strengthened.[27]

The obvious reason why the Church has so far refused to recognize the Catholic homophile community is the persistence of the traditional moral judgment concerning the homosexual. It is my personal belief and hope that the Church will undertake a serious reappraisal of its traditional moral judgment, especially since that judgment rests on extremely debatable grounds both in Scripture and tradition. Further, the potential contribution which the homophile community can make to the human and spiritual development of the human community as a whole is a resource which the Church desperately needs at this point in history.

Moral Norms and the Homosexual

Such an acceptance of the homophile community in no way implies that the Church must drop its divinely imposed task of upholding moral ideals in the area of sexual behavior. Rather, the Church must and should continue to uphold moral ideals for the truly human use of sex. However, it must not continue to confuse these moral ideals with the purely formal element of heterosexuality as such. As Thielicke points out:

> The primary moral problem in sexual relations is not sex within marriage versus sex outside of marriage, or sex within a heterosexual versus sex within a homosexual relationship. The problem is sex as a depersonalizing force versus sex as fulfillment of human relationship. Thus the important question would appear to be whether or not it is possible for the homosexual to achieve a responsible fulfilling relationship.[28]

The same moral norms should be applied in judging the sexual behavior of a true homosexual as we ordinarily apply to heterosexual activity. Negatively, any sexual activity that involves exploitation of another person is unequivocally to be condemned. As a Quaker study puts it:

This is a concept of wrongdoing that applies to both homosexual and heterosexual actions and to actions within marriage as well as outside of it. It condemns as fundamentally immoral every sexual action that is not, as far as humanly ascertainable, the result of mutual decision. It condemns seduction and even persuasion and every instance of coitus which, by reason of disparity of age or intelligence or emotional condition, cannot be a matter of mutual responsibility.[29]

From a positive viewpoint the will of God for human sexuality is an ideal state in which sexual activity would be entirely dominated and consecrated by mutual love and devotion. Such an ideal is seldom realized in its fullness even in heterosexual relationships within marriage. Selfishness is never completely absent from heterosexual relationships. Yet the inevitable presence of this factor within a sexual relationship does not lead the Church to condemn it and advise a married couple to refrain from sexual activity as sinful. Their sex can be justified insofar as it contributes to the development of a fulfilling and satisfying relationship based in mutual love.

From a moral viewpoint, however, a further problem exists concerning the individual's sexual development. Most moralists argue against moral culpability for a homosexual condition, since they presuppose that such a condition is the result of an unconscious psychological process which lies radically outside the conscious and, therefore, free self-determination of the individual. I am inclined to agree with this position. The majority of homosexuals seem to experience their condition as a given over which they have little or no conscious control. However, insofar as freedom and an element of conscious choice can or does enter into an individual's sexual orientation, to what extent is he morally free to choose a homosexual orientation?

Michael Buckley and other traditionalists believe that there is an element of choice and freedom in the sexual orientation of most homosexuals. They argue that insofar as human freedom and choice can enter into and influence one's sexual development, one is morally obliged to choose heterosexuality. Some moderns would argue, on the other hand, that insofar as freedom enters into the sexual identity, the ideal is not to choose either homosexual or heterosexual orientation, but to remain potentially bisexual in order to avoid the restrictions that necessarily accompany a choice of identity.

In contrast to both these positions, I believe that the moralist should emphasize the moral insight of Kierkegaard: the truly ethical question is not so much *what* you choose as it is *that* you choose. One begins to be ethical only after one has made a real commitment. Kierkegaard's point is that God as absolute value is never given to us as an object of choice. Rather, we can encounter the absolute only by committing ourselves absolutely to the relative. Saint John states forcibly that "God is love, and if any man loves he knows God." If true Christian and human love can exist equally in a homosexual or in a heterosexual context, then there is no a priori base for a moral choice between these contexts.

However, the real moral choice concerns committing or failing to commit ourselves to a fellow human being. Those persons who would deliberately remain at the immature stage of ambiguity in their sexual preferences will tend to remain uncommitted in their personal relationships. The failure to make a true commitment to another human person is, perhaps, the essential moral failing in all sexual relations, whether heterosexual or homosexual. We have already explored the prudential reasons for choosing a heterosexual orientation whenever that remains an open possibility. But the prior moral question is one of the quality of the commitment one makes to a fellow human person. Insofar as the subjective ambiguity of one's sexual preferences is used as a means of rationalizing a failure to commit oneself with fidelity in a genuine sexual love relationship, that ambiguity should be considered an amoral state. However, for one who enters actively into sexual relationships to maintain such an ambiguity in order to avoid commitment could represent an immoral choice.

As we have seen, there is a considerable body of evidence—the Hooker and Shofield studies, for example—that many homosexuals have avoided the trap of promiscuity and depersonalized sex by entering into a mature homosexual relationship with one partner with the intention of fidelity and mutual support. By means of this relationship they have not only escaped promiscuity in their relationship but have grown as human beings; they have learned to integrate their sexual impulses in a positive way into their personality, so that these impulses become no longer a negative, compulsive, and destructive force, but an instrument within their control for the expression of human love. Catholic homosexuals are well aware of their need for God's grace in order to remain faithful to their commitment and in order to grow in their power to express unselfish love. This is the motivation behind their seeking a liturgy of friendship. The Quaker committee, after a long study of homosexuality, drew the conclusion: "Surely it is the nature and quality of a relation that matters; one must not judge it by its outer appearance but its inner worth. Homosexual affection can be as selfless as heterosexual affection, and, therefore, we cannot see that it is in some way morally worse."[30]

Norman Pittenger, the noted Anglican theologian, believes that the primary spiritual problem that faces the Christian homosexual is his or her need, in Tillich's words, "to accept divine acceptance":

I should add that the homosexual who decided for a long relationship, as he may hope a life-long one, with another of his own sex, is almost certainly doing the very best thing that is open to him. Nor do I have the slightest doubt that God can and does bless the relationship. The basic question here for the homosexual is whether he will let the human love which to him is so wonderful find its grounding in the divine Love, in God himself. That it *is* so grounded I take to be a matter of fact, so far as Christian faith is concerned. . . .

But to *let* it be grounded, to allow it to be consciously realized and felt, requires human surrender. So I should ask the homosexual, "Will you *let* God bless you? Will you *let* him work in your life and in your friend's life and in the life you share together?"

God made men to become true lovers; he wants them to be the best they can possibly be. To acknowledge this and try to base one's existence and one's relationships on it, in full responsibility, gives that existence and that relationship a meaning and a dignity which otherwise they cannot have.[31]

The Positive Role of the Christian Homosexual Community

The militancy of the homosexual liberation movement has posed a new moral dilemma for the individual Christian homosexual. The "Gay Liberation" movement has placed a strong stress on the moral and social duty of homosexuals to "come out of the closet," to stop hiding their condition by conforming to an alien heterosexual image, and to proclaim themselves publicly as homosexual. Such a step, they claim, is necessary in order that individuals may win the freedom which will enable them to

commit themselves to public work for the social and political liberation of their homosexual brothers and sisters.

Christian homosexuals frequently find this stress particularly challenging, since it gives concrete expression to the
central Christian value of self-sacrificing love for one's
neighbor, especially the outcast and oppressed. They are
usually well aware that it is most often selfish fear and a
desire to escape personal humiliation, suffering, and loss
that motivates their desire to hide their identity.

One presiding officer in the Gay Activist Alliance confided to me that it was the Christian value of committing
oneself to help one's fellow human beings and the Christian hope of being able to derive strength for others from
one's own suffering and pain that originally led him into a
religious order as a novice, and which eventually led him to
take an active role in the gay liberation movement. A
surprising number of those Catholics who are active in the
movement come from a similar religious background. The
call to an open and honest proclamation of one's own
homosexuality and a commitment to work for the good of
the homosexual community strikes a deep, resonant chord
in the spirit of every committed Christian homosexual.

Such a public commitment has its obvious advantages;
for it frequently carries with it a deep experience of joyful
liberation, a freedom from the deceit and hypocrisy which
so frequently poison the lives of homosexuals. From their
sociological survey of thousands of male homosexuals in
three countries, Weinberg and Williams conclude that, all
other things being equal, coming out of the closet can be
psychologically healthier than trying to hide one's sexual
orientation. Looking at the question from a moral viewpoint, it can be said that if one has a clear choice between
two courses of action one of which is probably healthier
than the other, one has a clear moral obligation to choose
that course which offers the greatest promise of health. But

"coming out" carries with it many very serious difficulties as well. Perhaps the central problem is the consequences of a public proclamation for one's family and friends. Most Christian homosexuals have found it necessary to continue to conceal their sexual identity from their family because they are convinced that knowledge of their condition would cause their family untold pain and sorrow and no good would come of such a revelation. However, a *New York Times* article noted that among young homosexuals many are revealing their condition to their immediate family and finding acceptance and understanding. Perhaps the most successful and imaginative apostolate to the homosexual community undertaken by a priest is the effort of one priest in the Brooklyn diocese to organize the families of young homosexuals, who have been through the difficulties of accepting a homosexual son or daughter, so that they can help other parents through to acceptance and understanding.

Certainly, the Church should accept as one of its pastoral aims to help create such a relationship within the family. As we noted earlier, no greater disservice can be done to the family of a homosexual than to continue to insist on the unproven assumption that somehow the homosexuality of their child is due to a moral failing in the parental relationship. For such an insistence effectively blocks the possibility of young homosexuals' being able to be open with their parents in a spirit of love and understanding. Rather, stress should be placed on the obligation parents are under to accept a homosexual son or daughter with understanding and love. As I have already said, whenever one has the good fortune, in counseling, to encounter a psychologically healthy homosexual, aware of his or her own dignity and the capacity to love and be loved, one can be almost certain that that person's parents, whatever their disappointment over their child's condition, have responded to him or her with true acceptance and love.

Unquestionably, the ideal situation that should exist between the individual and his or her family is one of openness and acceptance. But there is no easy solution that can be given beforehand to any individual faced with the problem of revealing himself or herself to his family. I shall never forget the grief of a young man who, because he loved his parents very much and wished to spare them the grief of learning of his condition, had chosen to live in a distant city, when he received the following revelation at his father's funeral: before his death his father confided to a friend that he could not understand why his son had moved away, and felt that perhaps his son did not appreciate how much he loved him.

Two factors must be weighed by those individuals faced with this problem of self-revelation to their families. The first is the degree to which these individuals can foresee whether or not their parents can bring themselves to genuinely accept them with knowledge of their condition. Second, these individuals must estimate their own psychological strength. Will they be able to accept whatever happens in a spirit of understanding and compassion, and not react with bitterness and disillusionment?

Granting acceptance within one's family and by one's friends, there still remains the further challenge of deciding to play an active, public role for homosexual liberation. There surely are those among the Christian homosexual community whom God is calling to play a prophetic role in society in this regard. But here as in any prophetic role, such as the martyrs of old or the peacemakers of recent times, there must be a prudential and prayerful testing of spirits. The prophet must always pay a terrible price of personal suffering in order to bring about a true change in social attitudes. Before any individuals commit themselves to a public role, they must determine as best they can ahead of time what could be the worst things that could befall them: loss of their job, contempt and even hatred from society, personal injury, even prison, etc. And they must attempt to predetermine as best they can, based in their past experience and their self-knowledge, whether or not they have the interior strength to pass through such ordeals and come out a better human being because of them, and not cynical or bitter, a broken human being.

The prophetic function is essential if there is to be any advance in justice and charity toward the homosexual in the human community. Yet it can only be fulfilled under ordinary circumstances by someone who has the support of a loving community. Consequently a Christian community, such as Dignity, is essential to give the necessary human and spiritual support.

Another function which the Christian homosexual community can perform is that of providing role models. Homosexuals, especially the young, have a desperate need of models of what it means to live out a full human life as a homosexual. They especially need models of how to integrate spiritual and moral values into their life-style. One of the primary functions of social structure is to provide models for the young. The same social climate which forces homosexuals to hide their identity also effectively prevents any such role from being played within the ordinary structures of society. Consequently, there is need of a community within which the homosexual may encounter and come to know those who are sincerely trying to live such a human life with dignity.

One area in which the homosexual has a special need of both models and special counseling is in the realm of interpersonal relationships. The Church recognizes the need young heterosexuals have of special help in this area. Therefore, it has provided such services as pre-Cana and Cana conferences, and many forms of marriage and family counseling. A homosexual couple is even more desperately in need of such services. It is only within the context of a homosexual community that they could be provided.

The Accusation of Sexism

Richard McCormick, a moral theologian, states very clearly the primary objection of some moralists to a recognition by the Church of a homosexual community as such. He accepts the judgment of Francis Touchet:

> The homophile organizations (such as the Gay Liberation Front, Gay Activist Alliance, The American Church) ignore the prime focus on persons for a chosen focus on sexual preference and in doing so are guilty of an enslaving sexism.[32]

Consequently, McCormick views such organizations as jeopardizing an acceptance of the homosexual and as their own worst enemy because of their "monochromatic view." It must be conceded that any homophile organization that factually does focus exclusively on sexual preference and ignores the prime focus on persons would do a serious disservice to the homosexual, since homosexuals are frequently tempted to exaggerate the role that sexuality plays in life.

But I seriously question Touchet's assertion that such is the "chosen focus" of the organizations he names. First of all, the need for such homosexual organizations is based on the fact that the choice of a sexual focus and a sexual qualification of membership has already been made by society at large. There is at least an implicit, if not explicit, condition in most social institutions that one must be heterosexual in order to be accepted and fully participate in that institution. Nor is the Church exempt from such an exclusive condition. On the contrary, by viewing heterosexuality as the divine will and as "the ideal and the normal," as McCormick himself states, the Church has already set up a sexual condition which excludes the genuine homosexual from full participation in its structures. It makes no more sense to accuse the homosexual of an a priori chosen sexual focus than it would to accuse the blacks of a chosen skin-pigmentation focus or women's groups of a chosen biological focus. In each of these cases, as with homophile groups, the purpose of the group is to allow a focus on the person over against a denial of that focus by society at large.

Further, the fact is that the organizations Touchet mentions, although they do exist for those who are homosexually oriented, do not focus on sexuality as such. The Gay Liberation Front and the Gay Activist Alliance both are concerned with the transcendent personalist goals of justice and equality. The American Church has as its objective to make spiritual values and a life of worship available to the homosexual. Obviously, if the homosexual existed in an ideal human society where true justice and love were present there would be no need for such organizations. And, as we have seen, homophile organizations tend to see themselves as interim communities; their ideal is true integration of the homosexual as an equal into human society. But until the time that such an ideal can begin to be realized they have an essential role to play in its acquisition.

8

Conclusion: Justice, the Church, and the Homosexual

The 1971 International Synod of Catholic bishops issued a statement, *Justice in the World*, in which they emphasized that action for justice is an essential dimension of the Church's mission in the world:

> Action on behalf of justice and participation in the transformation of the world fully appears to us as a constitutive dimension of the preaching of the Gospel, or, in other words, of the Church's mission for the redemption of the human race and its liberation from every oppressive situation.[1]

A conclusion that would appear to follow from this study is that one of the "oppressive situations" which call for action on behalf of justice is the situation of the homosexual. Although in all likelihood the bishops of the world did not have the homosexual as such explicitly in mind when they drew up their statement, yet much of what they had to say about justice applies to the situation of the homosexual.

The bishops recognize that the message of love in the Gospel implies an absolute demand for the recognition of

191

the dignity and rights of one's neighbor. "Justice attains its inner fullness in love. Because every man is truly a visible image of the invisible God and a brother of Christ, the Christian finds in every man God himself and God's absolute demand for justice and love."[2] The message of the Christian homosexual community is that for the most part such a recognition has not been extended to the homosexual within the Christian community. The Synod insisted that, if the Church is to be credible when it speaks to the world, it first must be just itself in its own life. This practice of justice in its own life must begin with an unequivocal acknowledgment of, and respect for, the rights of all persons who together are the Church. "Within the Church rights must be preserved. No one should be deprived of his ordinary rights because he is associated with the Church in one way or another."[3] Again, Christian homosexuals believe that they have been deprived of their rights as a condition for their continued association with the Church. Among these rights are the right of association and the right to be heard in decisions which affect their lives.

The Synod acknowledges that frequently Christians simply do not see structured social injustices as sin. Consequently, they feel no obligation to do anything about them. As one commentary on the Synod document notes, we tend to ignore the fact that most of our personal choices occur within a societal framework which conditions, controls, and channels personal choice. So powerful and persuasive are these social situations that people frequently are not even conscious of their existence. They are inclined to see "laws of nature and of God" in what are purely human creations.[4] As a consequence Church members tend not to accept responsibility for the social structures which embody and make operational attitudes of prejudice and blindness. The homosexual community is inclined to see the unconscious univocal heterosexual structuring of society precisely as a human creation mistakenly accepted as the law of nature and of God which results in prejudice and blindness. Discrimination against women, the Synod acknowledges, has been structured unconsciously into the life and operation of the Church. As Archbishop Leo Byrne commented:

> Women are not to be excluded from any service of the Church, if the exclusion stems from questionable interpretation of Scripture, prejudice or blind adherence to merely human traditions that may have been rooted in the social position of woman in other times.[5]

If the findings of this study are correct, then the Church's attitude toward homosexuals is another example of structured social injustice, equally based in questionable interpretations of Scripture, prejudice, and blind adherence to merely human traditions, traditions which have been falsely interpreted as the law of nature and of God. In fact, as we have seen, it is the same age-old tradition of male control, domination, and oppression of woman which underlies the oppression of the homosexual.

When social structures oppress human dignity and freedom and maintain situations of gross inequality, the persons who share life within these situations also share responsibility for allowing them to continue. There is, then, a need and an obligation to undertake a process of consciousness-raising, whereby these injustices and the structures that support them can be identified. "Education . . . will awaken a critical sense, which will lead us to reflect on the society in which we live and on its values; it will make men ready to renounce these values when they cease to promote justice for all men."[6] Frequently in the past certain unjust social structures—slavery, for example—were defended and maintained because certain social values, such as stability and economic prosperity, were mistakenly understood as linked to the maintenance of these structures. In more recent times the inferior status of women is defended and maintained for the same reasons. But once the Church arrived at a clear consciousness that these supposed values were being maintained only by the perpetuation of essential injustice and disregard for the dignity and rights of certain of its members, it was obliged in conscience to reject these structures and do everything in its power to bring about a more just social order. The primary argument for the continued oppression of the homosexual is the belief, in reality unfounded, that the stability of the family and the moral health of society demand such an oppression. There is good reason to believe, as we have seen, that just the opposite is the case. It is the present oppressive situation which helps undermine the family structure by limiting the heterosexual to narrow and dehumanizing stereotypes and also by frequently forcing the homosexual into marriage. As Cardinal Carberry commented: "Help must be provided for the various minority peoples so that each group will not only acquire for itself that dignity and status in social life which is its due, but also will be able to enrich the other groups by the contribution of the riches that are inherent in its own character and culture."[7] Although Cardinal Carberry in all probability did not have the homosexual minority in mind, there is, as we have seen, a potential enrichment of society as a whole which would result from the homosexual community being helped to play its role in society in a constructive way.

All members of the Church are called on by the Synod to be prophetic in championing the rights of individuals and groups that are treated unjustly and in calling for an end to all forms of injustice. Participation by persons in the discourse which affects their lives and destinies is recognized by the Synod as a basic right and human need. There is a special need to implement that right within the Church itself so that everyone can be heard in a spirit of dialogue. The Synod made the point that the action of the Church is to be directed above all "to those men who because of various forms of oppression and because of the present character of Society are silent, indeed voiceless, victims of injustice."[8] This is certainly the situation of the Christian homosexual within the Church itself. Consequently, the Church authorities should recognize the same right for the Christian homosexual minority that the Synod proclaims for all minority groups, the right of association and the right to enter into dialogue with authorities and the rest of the community. All too often in the past, the Church and its moral theologians have made a priori statements concerning the morality and life-style of homosexuals without any serious effort at dialogue. In this area especially the words of Cardinal Dearden apply: "We must freely acknowledge that the Church must learn and not merely teach what is required in justice."[9] Homosexuals within the Church have an obligation, and therefore a right, to organize and attempt to enter into dialogue with Church authorities. Church authorities in turn should show an example in terms of just behavior toward the homosexual minority by displaying an active willingness to hear, to enter dialogue, and to seek ways to resolve whatever injustice becomes clear as a result of dialogue. It is only by means of such a dialogue that the Church can attain true consciousness of the injustices which the homosexual suffers and a real process can begin of separating the wheat from the chaff, the true implications of Christian faith and morality for the homosexual from the misunderstandings and prejudices of the past.

Epilogue

Three major theses have traditionally dominated the thinking of moral theologians concerning homosexuality. As we have seen, each one of these theses is open to serious question today. In fact, in each case a new understanding of human sexuality and new evidence concerning the lifestyle of homosexuals seem to support the contradictory thesis.

The first thesis is the traditional belief that the homosexual condition, and subsequently all homosexual activity, is contrary to the will of God. It was God's intention that all humans should be heterosexual. Consequently, we must search for an etiological explanation of the homosexual condition in sin, whether that be original sin, the sin of the parents, or the personal sin of the individual homosexual.

In contradiction to that thesis, I have argued that the homosexual condition is according to the will of God. God so created humans that their sexuality is not determined by their biology. We are born male and female; we become men or women by a process of education that is uncon-

196

scious for the most part. We now know from psychology that a homosexual phase is a normal phase of the sexual maturing process; that there is a homosexual as well as a heterosexual component in every human being; that always and everywhere a certain percentage of humans emerge from that complex learning process as predominantly homosexually oriented through no fault of their own. We have seen that in the light of today's knowledge of the Bible and of human sexuality, the traditional effort to prove from Scripture and from the natural law that such an orientation is contrary to the will of God no longer has any validity.

The second traditional thesis sprang from the first. Granted that the homosexual condition is contrary to the will of God, the presence of the homosexual in the human community is a menace to that community, and especially a threat to the values of the family. Consequently, everything should be done to isolate and "cure" the individual homosexual; or, failing that, to deny him or her any right to exercise their sexuality.

Over against that thesis I have proposed that, granted the homosexual is here according to God's will, God had a divine purpose in so creating human nature that a certain percentage of human beings are homosexual. In other words, homosexuals frequently are endowed with special gifts and a divinely appointed task in the construction of a truly human society. Rather than being a menace to the community in general and the family in particular, they have an important role to play in preserving and strengthening values such as interpersonal relations between the sexes and the development of a moral understanding of human sexuality outside the procreative context; values which are essential to the community and the family.

Finally, moral theologians have traditionally believed that the love which unites two homosexuals in a sexual union is a sinful love which separates them from the love of

God and places them in danger of eternal damnation. In recent times theologians have attempted to buttress that judgment with so-called empirical evidence coming from certain psychiatrists to the effect that homosexuals are necessarily mentally ill and all homosexual relationships are humanly destructive.

In contrast to that thesis—and perhaps most controversially—I have posed the thesis that there is the possibility of morally good homosexual relationships and that the love which unites the partners in such a relationship, rather than alienating them from God, can be judged as uniting them more closely with God and as mediating God's presence in our world. The new empirical evidence in support of this thesis is, first of all, the psychological evidence that homosexuality is not necessarily an illness and the empirical evidence that there are many homosexual couples in stable unions whose relationship provides the context for mutual growth and fulfillment. Further, there is evidence of the work of the Spirit bringing into existence believing communities of homosexuals who in a spirit of love and forgiveness are seeking dialogue with that same institutional Church which so often in the past and in recent times has been their persecutor.

I have been asked frequently to clarify further what I mean by "ethically responsible homosexual relationships." Obviously what I mean first of all is to distinguish between a homosexual relationship that is built on selfishness and mutual destructiveness and a relationship that is unselfish and constructive. I agree with Thielicke that the primary moral problem in sexual relationships is sex as a depersonalizing force versus sex as a fulfillment of human relationship.

Further, I do maintain that there are objective values and moral norms governing the constructive human use of sexuality. These norms are objective in the sense that they are intimately related to the nature of the human person as such, and thus have universal validity wherever there is growth toward the fullness of human personality. There are the negative norms involving a relationship based on the value of justice—e.g., any sexual relationship that involves exploitation of another person is immoral. The positive norms are based on the value of interpersonal love as the ideal human context for sexual expression. These positive norms must be derived from the concept of the human person as an end in himself, or herself, and from the necessary conditions of possibility for a genuine interpersonal love relationship. Among these conditions I personally believe are such norms as mutuality, fidelity, unselfishness, etc.

I hope in the near future to explore a new ethical understanding of human sexuality as a form of human play—where play is understood as any action which has its meaning in itself in the here-and-now; that is to say, an action that is end-in-itself, just as the person is end-in-himself or -herself.

Beyond these general principles I believe it is impossible for me at this point to define more clearly or to lay down a priori what the nature of an "ethically responsible homosexual relationship" should be. This is a task which necessarily must be reserved to the Christian homosexual community and its own communal discernment of its experience. As John Milhaven said in his letter concerning my manuscript to the *National Catholic Reporter*:

> If anything is clear about human sexuality, it is that Christians today are experiencing values in it that were generally unknown to the traditional Christian. . . . Can one presume that there are no similar developments in homosexual experience? Can one expound the "meaning of human sexuality" without having a clear

idea of what actually takes place in homosexual love in our culture? Can one pronounce moral judgments on homosexual behavior without ever taking a long, unblinking look at the actual experience of homosexual love in our times?

May more and more of the real experiences of Christian homosexuals find through brave men . . . expression in the forum of the Church. It is up to the Church, all of us, to speak and listen and gradually, carefully, form a helpful consensus on this agonizing question.

We will be doing only what the Christian community has done on troubling issues many times in the past.

Appendix 1:
Revisions of the Text

It is close to fifteen years since I first wrote the text of this book. When the possibility of republishing it arose, I gave the text a careful rereading to see what I would like to revise. I was surprised and delighted to find that the Introduction, part 1 on moral theology, and part 2 on the positive approach held up remarkably well. Apart from a few clarifications and some further evidence strengthening my original position, and some changes in language that now appears to me as sexist, there is very little that I would wish to add or revise. But the intervening fifteen years I have spent as a psychotherapist and as a minister to gay people have given me a different perspective on their pastoral needs. As a result there are many passages in part 3, Pastoral Ministry to the Homosexual Community, which I would revise or nuance in a different way. The first revision would be the title itself: there is no "homosexual" community, but there is a "gay" community. Homosexuality is a medical term for a sexual condition; whereas the word gay indicates positive self-acceptance, the only attitude on which community can be built.

In the section "The Goal of Heterosexual Adjustment" (pp. 162–67) I would profoundly disagree with the quotation from Hettlinger that one cannot be sure of one's sexual orientation until the age of twenty-five or later. After dealing with hundreds of gay people in in-depth psychotherapy and doing short-term counseling with several hundred others, I am now aware that most gay men were aware of their sexual orientation at a very early age. They may not have had a name for it, but they were aware of the difference. In fact, a large number were aware of their orientation in early childhood.

For this and other reasons I would no longer place the same emphasis on "exploring every avenue toward the achievement of normal heterosexual capacities and relationships." In all the case histories I have dealt with there was only one case of pseudohomosexuality, i.e., someone who feared they were homosexual whose true sexual orientation was heterosexual. After several years of therapy that person was able to make a successful heterosexual adjustment. But there were literally dozens of cases of pseudoheterosexuality—clients who attempted to deny or repress their homosexuality and live out a heterosexual life. I am certain that from a psychological perspective this is a much more serious problem for many people.

The major reason I offered the advice about making a heterosexual adjustment where possible was the extreme difficulty in the past of living out a homosexual life-style successfully. I made it quite clear that I understood these difficulties were "not necessarily due to homosexuality as such, but are the results of both society's and the Church's attitude to the homosexual." The remarkable advances made in the eighteen years since the Stonewall revolution have changed the situation drastically. The gay liberation movement has made a happy gay life in terms of civil rights, job security, and freedom from harassment a very real possibility.

There is a real gay human community, a strong, united community, ready to meet all the needs of lesbian women and gay men. Gays in New York City, for example, have established the Lesbian and Gay Community Services Center, a home that serves all members of the gay community. They have created SAGE (Senior Action in a Gay Environment) to help meet the needs of the older members. They have founded the Hetrick-Martin Institute for Gay Youth to help meet the social, medical, legal, and counseling needs of young gay people, which in turn brought into existence Harvey Milk High School for those students who could not survive and grow in the public school system. GMHC (the Gay Men's Health Crisis) has done a remarkable job of organizing to meet the critical health needs of the gay community, and of other groups as well, during the AIDS crisis. Many other excellent volunteer groups such as Persons with AIDS Coalition and the AIDS Resource Center are striving to meet the needs of people with AIDS, gay and straight, to the best of their ability. In fact, the gay community has developed an organizational structure of social services that will survive for generations of gay people yet to come.

There are hundreds of other organizations designed to meet the needs of gay people, among them the gay religious groups such as Dignity, Integrity, Metropolitan Community Church, the Gay Synagogue (Beth Sinhat Torah), Lutherans Concerned, Affirmation, and many, many others. There are also innumerable social groups, political groups, and artistic groups. Lesbians and gay men have formed a very real community of love, concern, and compassion.

I am much more aware now of how subtle forms of homophobia were operative in much of the professional advice given to young people about making heterosexual adjustment. It is clear that most people's sexual orientation is firmly established in early childhood. Once it is established, there is no way to change one's sexual orientation. After fifteen years of extensive therapeutic work with lesbian and gay clients, I would no longer claim that there is "a limited chance of therapeutic cure"; I now believe that it is impossible to change one's sexual orientation any more than one can change blue eyes to brown. The best response one can make to one's sexual orientation is to accept it and learn to live with it in the healthiest and most productive way possible.

The basic argument of the section entitled "The Case For and the Case Against Abstinence" (pp. 167–75) remains valid, namely, that a life of sexual abstinence is *not* a practical pastoral solution to the problems of lesbian women and gay men. I would, however, disagree today with the statement I made on page 168, that "a life of abstinence from all sexual experience . . . remains a good prudential choice for the homosexual in today's society." I am fully aware that the presence of AIDS gives the choice of abstinence a new priority. But in my experience as a psychotherapist, I have found that the vast majority of people living out a life of abstinence do so for pathological reasons. Many have interiorized the homophobia of the surrounding culture and the Church and as a consequence hate and fear their sexual feelings. Frequently these people are the most radical persecutors of other gays and lesbians. Others live out a life of abstinence because of serious trauma to their capacity for intimacy with another human.

I am aware that there are a few exceptional people who have a healthy sexual self-awareness and are capable of genuine intimacy who voluntarily choose a life of sexual abstinence. These people usually feel a call to religious life and ministry and see their life of abstinence as a special grace from God. Their attitude is quite different from those who seek to live out a life of abstinence compulsively because they see their sexual feelings as "objectively disordered" and any expression of them as "evil."

Those who have repressed or denied their homosexual feelings for pathological reasons are the ones in greatest danger of acting out those needs compulsively, imprudently, and unconsciously, seeking punishment for what they see as their crime. They, therefore, are in the greatest danger of being exposed to the AIDS virus.

I would certainly disagree with my statement, "The dangers and difficulties of an active homosexual life are so great and the probability that, owing to guilt and self-hatred, a homosexual relationship may prove destructive both to the individual and to the other person involved is so high, that every Christian homosexual may be well advised to try to structure his or her life without an active sexual relationship." On the contrary, today I would heartily advise all gay people to develop the most intimate and committed relationship possible for them. Where there is a problem with intimacy or interiorized self-hate, I would advise seeking out therapeutic help with a nonhomophobic therapist.

I still feel that the human ideal for all sexual expression is within the context of a monogamous, committed, faithful relationship. I do not see this, however, as imposing a heterosexual norm on gay people. I believe that we are dealing here with a fundamental human need that has to do with the development of trust and love and the greatest development of psychic maturity and health. However, I am also aware of the many people who are incapable, for whatever reason—psychological, social, or economic—of entering into such a relationship. The best these people are capable of is a "one-night stand" or an occasional sexual liaison with a friend. Such activity, however, should be prudent and follow the rules of "safer sex."

This shift in emphasis on the issue of abstinence also corresponds to a shift in my theological understanding of sexual sin. I now believe that the most serious sexual sin is alienation from and suppression of God's good gift of sexuality. I am inclined to agree with Norman Pittenger that there are only three kinds of sexual activity between consenting adults: "good, better and best sex." These themes will be fully developed in my new book, *Taking a Chance on God: Spiritual Messages to a Gay Christian.*

Appendix 2:
Some Pastoral Reflections on AIDS

When this book was initially written about fifteen years ago, the world, to my knowledge, was completely unaware of AIDS. I intend to treat all the issues involved with AIDS, its challenge and meaning for the gay community, more extensively in a book to be published soon, *Taking a Chance on God: Spiritual Messages to a Gay Christian*. But I could not reissue this book without sharing a few thoughts about AIDS, especially in a pastoral context.

Some Theological Reflections on AIDS[1]

First of all let me make an apodictic theological statement: *it is not God's will that anyone have AIDS*. It is not punishment for sin. Among the many voices being raised in the churches today, there are some who would have us identify the AIDS epidemic with God's vengeance on the homosexual community. The judgment implicit in such a viewpoint is that all homosexual activity is "sinful," a judgment that this book has, I believe, called into question and successfully repudiated. Those who make such a claim

207

betray a fundamental misunderstanding and distortion of the Christian revelation concerning the nature of God. Amid the trappings of theology and piety, such voices frequently reveal homophobic prejudices and thinly veiled hatred of gay men and lesbian women.

The God whom Jesus revealed is a loving and merciful parent, not one who punishes children like a wrathful father or a vengeful mother, especially for something over which they have no choice: "You did not receive a spirit of slavery bringing fear into your life again, but a spirit of adoption by which you can cry out: Abba [Father, Mother]" (Rom. 12:15). Jesus specifically repudiated the pagan notion that God inflicts physical punishment on earth for supposed sin (cf. Lk. 13), and strongly condemned the pagan worship of God out of superstitious fear. The worshipers of Baal, for example, were obliged to cast their firstborn into the flames before Baal's statue in order to escape being punished by disease and famine. Some preachers today demand that gay people throw a life of sexual intimacy into the fire before a vindictive God in order to avoid divine punishment. When some friends of Jesus asked about a particular victim of disease, "Who sinned, this man or his parents?" Jesus answered: "Neither. The works of God will be made manifest in him" (Jn. 9:2–3).

The mistake made by Jesus' friends here was in assuming a direct cause-and-effect connection between one's moral choices and one's circumstances. Jesus points out that reality is not that simple; he speaks of a God who lets the sun shine on the good and the bad alike and who gives rain to those who do good as well as those who do evil. In his own day Jesus responded to those whose suffering was most conspicuous, namely the lepers, not with righteous judgment but with compassion. When he met the victims of leprosy (which was for his time and place what AIDS is for us), he listened to them, touched them, healed them (see Mk. 1:40–45; Lk. 17:11–19).

Many fundamentalists, using the myth of Sodom and Gomorrah as an analogy, see AIDS as God's punishment. They persist in interpreting the sin of Sodom and Gomorrah as homosexuality and ignore the clear reference in Scripture to the sin of inhospitality. Ezekiel, in fact, is clear that the sin for which Sodom and Gomorrah was punished by the Old Testament God was the failure of a wealthy society to provide for the poor: "They lived in pride, and plenty and in thoughtless ease. They supported not the poor and the needy . . ." (Ez. 16:49–50). The real sodomites in our own time are those whose greed and quest for power have brought war and poverty to millions of innocent people. Obviously God has not perfected a new disease to inflict on them.

Those who identify AIDS as God's punishment of homosexuals run the risk of placing themselves in a spiritually dangerous state by separating themselves from those they call sinners. They exhibit the arrogance of the Pharisee who boasted, "I am not a sinner"; while the publican genuinely prayed: "Lord, be merciful to me, for I am a sinful man." "Do not judge," Jesus said, "and you shall not be judged."

The AIDS epidemic is another graphic example of the mystery of evil and suffering. Throughout Sacred Scripture, from Genesis to Revelation, the most puzzling question is why the wicked prosper and the innocent suffer. We face this same question today.

The AIDS epidemic challenges all of us to reaffirm our faith and trust in God as a loving parent in whom love and mercy, justice and peace embrace. It challenges us to do all we can to relieve the suffering of those afflicted, and to hope and pray that somehow out of the suffering and evil involved, God will bring about greater good.

Ministers of the Gospel should, then, refrain from judgments which, far from expressing the good news of salvation, serve only to increase fear and prejudice. They should also advocate and lobby for adequate funds to support the kind of research that will discover a cure for AIDS. Finally, they should seek the training and expertise that will allow them to minister more effectively to persons with AIDS. Those who seek to help gay people with AIDS must first of all ferret out the homophobia hidden deep in their own psyches. They must also deal on a profound level with their own fears of disease and death. Finally, they must reject the notion of a vindictive God who must be worshiped out of fear.

People with AIDS need above all else someone who is not afraid to touch them; someone willing to listen and who won't run away when they need to ventilate their anger or when they need to share their fear and despair. As Jesus asked his disciples, "Could you not watch one hour with me?" (Mk. 14:37).

The Impact of AIDS on the Gay Community

One question that has not yet been dealt with appropriately concerns the impact of AIDS on the consciousness of the gay community. After centuries of oppression and alienation, lesbians and gay men in the past fifteen years have won through to an extraordinary degree of healthy self-acceptance and political freedom. The AIDS epidemic threatens to wipe out all these gains by creating an atmosphere of hysteria and fear that could drive gay people back into the closet.

The greatest threat to our liberation as gay people is fear. Fear can render us suspicious, create divisions among us, impoverish our conscience, and cripple our response to those around us. Fear deadens the soul and diminishes our capacity for love. Consequently, the gay community must fight not to be ruled by fear; we must realize that violence, long before it touches our bodies, first destroys the spirit of its victims through fear. From my own experience as a prisoner of war in Germany during World War II, I came to the conclusion that fear is the primary weapon that evil people use to manipulate the good and prevent their liberation. We gay people must remember that true liberation comes from within ourselves and not from without. Only after we have freed ourselves from the control of fear will we find the courage to listen to the voices of the oppressed around us and the freedom to act for human rights and equality.

AIDS represents a special threat to the faith and hope of those religious believers among lesbians and gay men who have sought to combine their religious faith with their self-acceptance as gay. There has always been a high degree of religious consciousness in the gay community which has expressed itself in a faith and hope in God despite all oppression, even that fostered by the human church. The AIDS crisis is a fundamental challenge to that faith and trust. Many gays who persist in their religious belief are in danger of returning to a belief in a demonic God of fear, who, having created certain humans gay, then threatens them with hideous death at an early age because of their sexuality. There is a struggle going on in the religious gay community to hold onto a sense of healthy self-acceptance while maintaining a fundamental faith and trust in God.

The first reaction of the gay community to AIDS has been a reevaluation of its efforts to achieve sexual liberation. There has been an end to the all-out celebration of sexuality and the constant exploration of new forms of sexual fulfillment. There is a new emphasis on prudence in all sexual expression. And there is a new exploration of the kind of committed relationship that is appropriate to lesbian women and gay men and is not merely an imitation of heterosexual conventions. In gay newspapers the majority of ads seeking sexual partners are now found in the section entitled "For Lovers Only." The danger in this reaction is that the gay community could lose the freshness and joy of its celebration of God's gift of sexuality and revert to feelings of alienation from and loathing for sex.

Gay sex came out of the closet with the Stonewall revolution; a paradoxical result of the AIDS crisis is that it has brought gay love out of the closet. Before AIDS, the only visible members of the gay community were those who frequented the gay discos, bars, and baths. Those who were involved in loving, committed relationships remained closeted to protect each other's jobs, homes, and families from the consequences of public disclosure. But now AIDS has forced many couples to acknowledge their relationships. I know hundreds of ministers, hospital personnel, and families who have been astonished at the depth of love, support, and self-sacrifice that characterizes so many gay couples.

There is a spirituality of compassion intimately present in the gay and lesbian community, where many thousands are involved in service to persons with AIDS, whether by bringing food and lending solace in visits to the afflicted or by other compassionate actions. In fact, I see the extraordinarily loving response of the lesbian and gay community to its brothers and sisters in need as one of the greatest outpourings of spiritual love in our times.

In his book *AIDS: The Spiritual Dilemma*,[2] John Fortunato offers a provocative and creative insight into the question, What good can come of AIDS? Starting from the assumption that God in her goodness always brings even greater good from all evil, John finds part of the answer to his question in the idea of "Proclaiming the Good News of Mortality." It always has been the prophetic role of gay men and lesbians to lead the Church and Western culture toward an acceptance of embodiment, a sense of identity with the body and its sensuousness. We must let our "word become flesh." We must give up the dualistic, escapist concept that we are immortal souls encased in a mortal body which we use but are not identified with. However, when we celebrate the sacredness of physical creation and affirm the body, we immediately face the reality of death.

Our culture has perfected its techniques of denying death and has thus created an atmosphere of pseudo-immortality. Fortunato quotes Karl Rahner as saying: "Time becomes madness if it cannot reach fulfillment. To be able to go on forever would be a hell of empty meaninglessness. No moment would have any importance because one could postpone and put everything off until an empty later which would always be there."[3] There could be no greater curse than to be denied the right to die.

Since time immemorial gay people have represented mortality to the world because the chief escape from mortality was through procreation. This is why the greatest curse in ancient times was barrenness. This is also why Isaiah predicts that, after the Messiah comes with the gift of resurrection in the flesh, "even the Eunuchs who observe the sabbath and resolve to do what pleases me and cling to my covenant, I will give, in my house and within my walls, a monument and a name better than sons and daughters. I will give them an everlasting name that shall never be cut off" (56:4–6). In Matthew 19:12 Jesus makes it clear that the term eunuch applies to all those who are sexually different and who, for whatever reason, do not procreate. Finally, in Acts 8:26, the Holy Spirit leads Philip out into the desert to baptize a eunuch whom Philip finds reading Isaiah—the same prophet who foretold that all who are sexually different will have a special place in the house of the Lord. This prophecy is being fulfilled today within the gay Christian movement.

Today, with the onset of the AIDS epidemic, we who are gay and who at some subliminal level have always intimated death to the world at large are now linked to a frightening, usually fatal disease. By our very existence on two major accounts we are a constant reminder to everyone of the inevitability of death. Gay people, who have long proclaimed at least half the truth of mortality—through our voracious appetite for an embodied life and by showing the sanity of living out an embodied but limited life as fully as we can—are now called on to give a special witness to the meaning of death. In an attempt to articulate the nonrational meaning of AIDS, Fortunato declares: "If our journey with AIDS serves to bring us all home to the grand and the grave, the joyful and sobering truth of mortality; if this suffering helps heal the madness of an eternally empty later whose existence we have duped ourselves into believing in; if this nightmare brings back to our consciousness the resurrection hope without which life is just so much courageous despair, then in the groaning of creation, with tears and sighs, perhaps the Holy Spirit will usher in some modicum of peace or even a corner of salvation that might otherwise have been unattainable. And in that travail, perhaps . . . perhaps we will glimpse the meaning of AIDS for our spiritual journey."[4]

In a recent interview in the *New York Times* (15 July 1987), a gay man in San Francisco summed up the effect of the AIDS crisis on the gay community: "So much of our lives are dedicated to dealing with death, taking care of our friends who are dying. Gays are feeling the importance of being alive, of saying things that might not otherwise be said. We're taking care of each other, and nothing is taken for granted. We're doing everything we can to take care of our own. We're not happy, but we are not wimping out. Anyone who thinks gays are sissies should take a look. We have developed enormous strengths." Because we do not attempt to escape mortality through procreation or by rejecting a fully embodied life, gay people have no other choices except despair or to trust in God's power and promise and become a resurrection people.

Appendix 3:
A History of
the Publication of This Book

This section provides a history of the conflicts within the Society of Jesus and especially with the Vatican Congregation for the Doctrine of the Faith concerning the publication and promotion of this book. The appendix consists of three parts: part 1 dates from the first publication of the book, 15 January 1976, and recounts my initial four-year effort in dealing with censors from among my fellow moral theologians both here in the United States and in Rome, an effort which eventually resulted in the book's receiving official permission to be published. Part 2, which was added nine years later in May 1985, recounts the process through which the Vatican removed the permission to publish and ordered me to be silent on the issue of homosexuality. Part 3 was written in July 1987 and recounts the events that resulted in my decision to speak and publish once again on the subject of homosexuality after ten years of silence; a decision that led to my expulsion from the Society of Jesus and the denial of my legal right in the Catholic Church to exercise my priesthood.

Part 1: Permission Is Granted

The history of how I came to write this book and what happened in the process of seeking publication will, I believe, be of interest to the reader and shed some light on the difficulty of fostering an intelligent and open discussion on the subject of homosexuality, especially within the Church. As C. A. Tripp observed of society at large, in the chapter on politics and homosexuality in his recent book *The Homosexual Matrix*, there is "a fiercely dangerous set of emotions that has proved itself capable of corrupting every channel of enlightenment and of suppressing information that would ultimately be useful to everyone's understanding of himself and the world around him" (New York: McGraw-Hill, 1975). A concerted effort was made within certain sectors of the Church to prevent this book from seeing the light of day. But, thank God, the convictions of reasonable, courageous men prevailed, and as a result this book can now be published with an official *imprimi potest*.

The history of my manuscript began when I published a series of three articles entitled "The Christian Male Homosexual" in the *Homiletic and Pastoral Review* in 1970. These articles were well received, and their enthusiastic reception led me to believe that the time was ripe for a full-scale, book-length study of the moral and pastoral issues of homosexuality. A first draft of the book was ready for publication in 1972 and I began my search for a publisher.

On Labor Day weekend in 1973 I gave the keynote speech at the first national convention of Dignity, an organization for Catholic homosexuals. That speech, which represented a summary statement of the manuscript, was subsequently published in the 5 October 1973 issue of the *National Catholic Reporter*. The response was staggering.

Literally hundreds of letters poured into my office, mostly from priests and religious who were attempting to counsel homosexuals, asking advice and inquiring about the manuscript of the forthcoming book. In January of 1974 I had an offer of publication from Sheed and Ward.

Almost simultaneously with the offer of publication I received a notice from my Jesuit superiors that Father General Pedro Arrupe, S.J., had written from Rome ordering me not to publish anything in the popular press and not to address homosexual groups. (At a later date, officials told me that with the appearance of the article in the *National Catholic Reporter*, pressure was brought to bear on Father General by various Roman Congregations to take some action against me in the matter.) I was particularly upset by this prohibition, first because the implication of the letter that the moral debate could be carried on outside the notice of the public media and exclusively on a peer-group level seemed to me to be totally impracticable; and secondly because I was convinced that it was only through open discussion, with the Catholic homosexual community participating as an equal partner, that any real advance could be made in the Church's moral understanding of homosexuality and consequent pastoral practice.

In the meantime, while participating in an all-day seminar on Christian sexuality sponsored by the Newark diocese of the Episcopal Church, I was asked a question concerning homosexual marriages. I was erroneously reported in a church magazine, the *Living Church*, as approving "the liturgical solemnification of homosexual marriages." When this report reached Rome, pressure was again brought to bear on Father General. A second letter arrived in which I was forbidden to speak, publish, or teach anything on the question of homosexuality until a commission of theologians had examined my teaching.

A commission was set up, and reports were received from my fellow Jesuit theologians Avery Dulles, Richard McCormick, and Robert Springer. Charles Curran of Catholic University and an outstanding biblical scholar who has asked to remain anonymous also did reports. Although they did not necessarily agree with my arguments and conclusions, yet, I understand, a majority of the commission reported that they found the manuscript a serious and scholarly work worthy of publication. Several felt strongly that there should be a public debate on all the issues involved and that my manuscript would be an important contribution to that debate. One man even urged as a matter of principle that I should publish the book without submitting it to any form of prior censorship.

The commission's report was forwarded to Father Arrupe in Rome. He responded in April 1974, saying he was grateful for the report of the commission but felt that a further step was needed. Since circumstances had focused personal responsibility on him to stress the need for me to be sensitive to the traditional norm of morality in my treatment of homosexual conduct, he requested that I forward a copy of my manuscript to Rome, so that he could review it personally.

After waiting five months for an answer from Rome, I found out that the manuscript never reached the Father General's desk, but was lost in a secretary's desk drawer. I was then told that I should revise the manuscript in the light of the criticism received from the commission and send a second, revised version to Rome. After various delays a final revised copy of the manuscript was sent to Rome in 1975. A reply was finally received in October. In his reply Father Arrupe turned over authority to give a "permission to publish" to the Provincial of the New York Province of the Society of Jesus. He stated that he would not object to publication granted that certain suggestions and guidelines be accepted and followed. Among the guidelines suggested was that another biblical scholar be consulted. In fulfillment of that request, I sent the manuscript to William Thompson, S.J., of the Jesuit School of Theology in Chicago.

Father General also requested, among other things, that I make clear where my manuscript differs from the traditional teaching of the Church. After some negotiations with Father Eamon Taylor, S.J., the New York provincial, I made the additions and corrections suggested. The *imprimi potest* was important to me, first of all, because it is my hope that this book will help foster an all-out discussion of the Church's moral understanding and pastoral practice concerning the homosexual. Secondly, I particularly want to reach, and open up new, hopeful possibilities for, all those Catholic homosexuals who are struggling to put together their dual identities as Catholics and homosexuals. Therefore it was important to me that the book should be accepted into the mainstream of Catholic debate and reflection.

The appearance of the document from the Sacred Congregation for the Doctrine of the Faith, "Declaration on Certain Questions Concerning Sexual Ethics," in January 1976, called into question once again the granting of permission to publish. I informed my superiors how I would respond to the Declaration in my book and was delighted to receive a letter from the provincial, Father Eamon G. Taylor, S.J., on 28 January 1976, saying: "in my opinion the adjustments you have made in your manuscript in accordance with the agreements reached in our conversation of November 10 are responsive to the recommendations of Fr. General's letter of September 19, and . . . as a result, I am happy to be able to grant the *imprimi potest*, as of this date."

It is important for the reader to understand what is implied in the granting of an ecclesiastical *imprimi potest*, i.e., permission to publish, by my religious superiors and what is not implied. First, the authorities that grant the permission in no way commit themselves as agreeing or disagreeing with the content of the book. Rather, all that is implied is that authorities have assured that the book is a prudent work that meets the standards of scholarship for publication of a book on a controversial moral topic. Secondly, the "permission to publish" in no way implies that the conclusions stated in this book are accepted by the Catholic Church as part of its official teaching; only the Pope and the Bishops have the authority to teach officially in the name of the Church.

Consequently, the conclusions arrived at in this book are my personal opinions and their only authority is the value of the reasoning and evidence that I can bring to support them and the confirmation they find in the reader's experience and observations.

I hasten to assure my readers that at no point have I been asked to change or in any way alter my insights or convictions in order to receive official permission to publish. On the contrary, after receiving the critical comments of the various readers, I have been able to strengthen the manuscript and sharpen my position, with the result that the book is, I believe, a much better book.

I especially want to thank all those who generously and courageously sponsored me through these years of patience and trial, especially Robert J. O'Connell, S.J., who acted as my intermediary with Rome, and Robert Springer, S.J., who was a particularly valued consultant and friend; also Robert Carter, S.J., and the members of the New York Chapter of Dignity who prayed, sorrowed, and rejoiced with me as we went through the ups-and-downs of seeking permission from the Church to publish.

15 January 1976
Crossroads of Reflection and Action
New York, N.Y.

Part 2: *Ordered to Silence*

Much water has gone under the bridge since I finished the preface in 1976. I would like to update my reader on the history of the book, especially its vicissitudes with the Vatican since its initial publication. Nearly two years after the publication of my book, I was notified by my provincial that the Vatican Congregation for the Doctrine of the Faith had sent a letter to the Jesuit superior general, Pedro Arrupe, S.J., regarding the book. The Congregation ordered that the *imprimi potest* be removed from future editions of the book and also that I was not to give future lectures on homosexuality or sexual ethics. I would like to share with my readers the text of that letter which I first saw when it was released by the Vatican several months later to be published in the magazine *Origins* (vol. 6, pp. 612–15). The letter explains the reasons why the Congregation made the decision to remove the *imprimi potest* and silence me.

I

The congregation first intends to clarify certain points concerning the nature and publication of this book.

1. The book, *The Church and the Homosexual*, clearly and openly advocates a moral position regarding homosexuality which is contrary to—in theory as well as in practice—the traditional and actual teaching of the church.

In his own words, the author presents an "advocacy theology" (p. 24) for "ethically responsible homosexual relationships" (p. 199 and *passim*). The contents of this book are arranged to show that there is no proven moral obligation to refrain from "ethically responsible homosexual relationships" and that, therefore, both church and civil norms must accept these relationships as legitimate. The author describes the spirit and content of the book in the following words:

"In their traditional presentation of moral obligation, Aquinas and Alphonsus Liguori, among others, always maintained *nulla obligatio nisi sit certa*. Given, as I believe, (1) the uncertainty of clear scriptural prohibition, (2) the questionable basis of the traditional condemnation in moral philosophy and moral theology, (3) the emergence of new data which upset many traditional assumptions, and (4) controversies among psychologists and psychiatrists concerning theory, etiology, treatment, and so on, there obviously is a need to open up anew the question of the moral standing of homosexual activity and homosexual relationships for public debate" (cf. p. 21).

2. The book was published with the *imprimi potest* of the Jesuit provincial superior, Father Eamon Taylor; the *imprimatur* was not requested because, according to the judgment of the canonist consulted, "permission is recommended but not prescribed," and in this case "the purpose of the recommendation has already been fulfilled through the extensive process of examination. . ., and the further delays which would be entailed in requesting diocesan approval would constitute a disproportionate inconvenience to the author, the publisher. . . ."

This point is important: What is the *purpose* of the *imprimi potest* which was given? Although the *imprimatur* is strongly recommended in a case of this sort (cf. this Congregation's *Decretum de Ecclesiae Pastorum vigilantia circa libros* of March 19, 1975), it is not required; the permission of the competent superior, however, is required according to the constitutions of the Jesuit Order. The *imprimi potest* given would normally indicate that the contents of the book were judged to be sound, in accord with the church's teaching, and safe to follow in practice. This is clearly not the case with Father McNeill's book.

Father McNeill explains in the Preface to his book his understanding of the significance of the *imprimi potest:*

"It is important for the reader to understand what is implied in the granting of an ecclesiastical *imprimi potest,* i.e., permission to publish, by my religious superiors and what is not implied. First, the authorities that grant the permission in no way commit themselves as agreeing or disagreeing with the content of the book. Rather, all that is implied is that authorities have assured that the book is a prudent work that meets the standards of scholarship for publication of a book on a controversial moral topic. Secondly, the 'permission to publish' in no way implies that the conclusions stated in this book are accepted by the Catholic Church as part of its official teaching; only the Pope and the Bishops have the authority to teach officially in the name of the Church." (cf. pp. 221–22)

Normally, however, the *imprimi potest* is the superior's permission based on the censor's judgment that the book does not contain errors or advice which would be harmful to its readership.

For this reason, it seems important to note the explanation given by the provincial superior, Father Eamon G. Taylor, S.J., in granting the *imprimi potest.* His reason in departing from the customary norms governing the granting of the *imprimi potest* seems to be based on the fact that he envisions a *restricted readership* for the book—one for whom the danger of scandal could be reasonably said not to exist. Father Taylor's prepared statement on his *imprimi potest* stated:

"The permission to publish granted by ecclesiastical superiors does not imply any judgment of the content or opinions expressed in the book. It does imply that the work has been judged competently and responsibly written, and therefore, *suitable for presentation to and evaluation by scholars.* . . . The ultimate judgment upon Father McNeill's method and conclusion will come from *his peers among professional moral theologians*, and from the magisterial authority of the church, to which Father McNeill defers" (italics ours).

In this explanation, Father Taylor appeals to "scholars" and "peers" in the field of moral theology as the intended readership justifying the permission to publish.

On the other hand, it seems apparent to us that the kind of scholarly and peer-group readership envisioned by the provincial superior was not at all the audience Father McNeill and his publishers had in mind. We conclude this both from his stated intention in the Preface of his book, and from the speeches and lectures he has given in city after city to promote the book's sale and its thesis on homosexuality. The intention of Father McNeill is clear; he says:

"The *imprimi potest* was important to me, first of all, because it is my hope that this book will help foster an all-out discussion of the Church's moral understanding and pastoral practice concerning the homosexual. Secondly, I *particularly want to reach, and open up new, hopeful possibilities for, all those Catholic homosexuals* who are struggling to put together their dual identities as Catholics and as homosexuals. Therefore it was important to me that the book should be accepted into the *mainstream of Catholic debate* and reflection" (p. 221, italics ours).

Father McNeill further indicated his intention of giving the widest possible publicity to his theological and pastoral opinions, when he comments on the developments leading up to publication in this way:

"Almost simultaneously with the offer of publication I received a notice from my Jesuit superiors that Father General Pedro Arrupe, S.J., had written from Rome ordering me not to publish anything in the popular press and not to address homosexual groups. (At a later date, officials told me that with the appearance of the article in the *National Catholic Reporter*, pressure was brought to bear on Father General by various Roman congregations to take some action against me in the matter.) I was particularly upset by this prohibition, first because *the implication of the letter that the moral debate could be carried on outside the notice of the public media and exclusively on a peer-group level* seemed to me to be totally impracticable; and secondly because I was convinced that it was *only through open discussion*, with the Catholic homosexual community participating as an equal partner, that any real advance could be made in the Church's moral understanding of homosexuality and consequent pastoral practice" (p. 219; italics ours).

Father McNeill indicates he took the attitude of some of the scholars on the commission which the Jesuit authorities set up to judge his work as encouragement to pursue a course of publicizing his ideas among the entire Catholic and secular community, rather than aim for the community of scholarship:

"a majority of the commission reported that they found the manuscript a serious and scholarly work worthy of publication. Several felt strongly that *there should be a public debate* on all the issues involved and that my manuscript would be an important contribution to that debate" (p. 220).

It seems clear that Father Taylor's stated purpose and the purpose and course of action of Father McNeill do not coincide. Therefore, even apart from a judgment about the wisdom of granting the *imprimi potest* in the first place, it seems altogether reasonable and necessary to withdraw it now.

3. We find it extraordinary that a book so clearly contradicting the moral teaching of the church would be published a few days after the publication of *Persona humana*, a document of this congregation treating in part of the same question; no reasonable person could imagine that time for serious study and evaluation had been given to the declaration of the authentic magiste-

rium of the church in this case. Such an action cannot
but indicate the gravest sort of disregard for the mature
study of and loyal support for the teachings of the
church expected of her sons, especially those who have
positions of responsibility through the reception of
holy orders. The following extract from the article in
Time magazine (Sept. 20, 1976) is an example of how
well this situation is understood by society at large:

"When the Congregation for the Doctrine of the Faith
issued its 5,000-word statement on homosexuality, premarital sex, and masturbation, it was responding in part
to complaints that the church was not providing sufficient
guidelines for sexual behavior and attitudes. Days later,
Father John McNeill, a Jesuit priest and former teacher
of moral theology at the now defunct Woodstock College
and at Fordham University, won the designation *imprimi
potest* (it can be printed) for a book strongly attacking the
church's views on homosexuality."

4. Finally, we think it important to clarify the issue
regarding the scandal caused by this book. This scandal comes from the content of the book itself—ideas
and suggested pastoral practice clearly at variance with
the teaching and practice of the church; from the circumstances of publication—the *imprimi potest* gives
the aura of ecclesiastical approval, and the publication
of the book within days after *Persona humana* gravely
damages the respectful attitude toward the teaching of
the authentic magisterium of the church in the public
view; and from the publicity and promotion given to
the book and its ideas by Father McNeill himself
through his tour of public lectures and press conferences.

One measure of the seriousness of this scandal is the
extraordinary step taken by the president of the episcopal conference in the United States, Archbishop Joseph
Bernardin of Cincinnati, on the occasion of the publicity given to Father McNeill's scheduled appearance in
his archdiocese:

"This weekend Father John McNeill, S.J., will be in the city to speak about his new book, *The Church and the Homosexual.* Because his visit has already been given public notice and because his lecture will also be given publicity, I wish to restate the church's position regarding homosexuality so there will be no confusion in the minds of people . . . No one can take it upon himself to alter this clear teaching. While it is legitimate for theologians to explore this moral question like any other, it is a disservice to challenge this teaching publicly in such a way as to give the impression that some radical change has taken place or is about to take place."

Such appearances by Father McNeill in various cities throughout the United States continue to be a source of scandal, both in the false hopes given to Catholic homosexuals and in the confusion caused in the community at large. These public appearances clearly indicate that the purpose originally stated for granting the *imprimi potest* by Father Taylor—"its presentation to and evaluation by scholars"—has long been set aside.

II

After the explicit clarification of the facts of the case by the above considerations, we are best able to address the second point: What steps or actions would be suitable to avoid further scandal? It seems to us that the following actions should be taken as a minimum:

1. Father Taylor should be required to withdraw the *imprimi potest*, so that it would not appear in any possible second printing, second edition, or translation of the book. It is clear that more than adequate distribution has already been given for purposes of scholarly study of the book.

2. It is important that the withdrawal of the *imprimi potest* and the reasons for it be communicated both to

Father McNeill and to the publisher of the book lest a situation develop again in which the fact that preparations had advanced so far might prompt local authorities to concede a further printing (edition or translation) with ecclesiastical approval.

3. It seems urgent that Father McNeill be prohibited from any further appearance or lecture on the question of homosexuality and sexual ethics, or in promotion of the book.

Directed at the time I received this from the Vatican through my provincial, I decided to comply with it and to the best of my ability I have tried to live up to these restrictions. I have not, however been denied the right to continue my direct ministry to lesbians and gay men.

At the time I was silenced I sent an open letter to the Dignity convention being held in Chicago, explaining why I chose to obey and had cancelled my scheduled speech:

I think it is important to note immediately what is not being said in the directive. It does not in any way demand a retraction or a repudiation of my ideas or judgments in this book. After a great deal of prayer and consultation I personally have made the decision to obey the directive. It was always my hope and dream that through my scholarship and efforts, I could make some contribution to a reconciliation of the Church with the gay community and the gay community with the Church. At this time and under these circumstances I now judge that the best contribution I can make to that dream is by my silence. I hope by my silence to be of service both to the Church which I love and the gay community with which I have become so closely identified.

I hope also that my silence will be eloquent. I hope it will join the silence of those many theologians and philosophers of pre-Vatican II, Maurice Blondel, Teilhard de Chardin, John Courtney Murray, Henri de Lubac, and many others whose obedience eventually led to their vindication. I would like my silence in some way to symbolize the defenseless silence through the centuries, and even today, of hundreds of thousands of gay Catholics.

John J. McNeill
15 May 1985

Part 3: *The Denial of the Right to Minister*

The final series of events that led to my expulsion from the Society of Jesus and my freedom once again to republish this book began with the Dignity convention in New York City in August 1985. This was the seventh biannual convention and the seventh at which I was invited to speak. I gave a talk entitled "New Dimensions of Christian Freedom" in which I dealt with such topics as the freedom to be "born again," the freedom to play, freedom of conscience, and the role of human freedom at the moment of death. I was very careful to abide by the guidelines I had received from the Vatican, so I did not address the issue of homosexuality directly. For over ten years I had been walking a difficult path between the impersonal and, as they appeared to me, insensitive directives I had received from Rome and the sufferings and needs of the lesbian women and gay men whom God had called me to serve. I had done the best I could to uphold the responsibility I owed to the Church as well as that I owed to my gay brothers and sisters. Never once in those ten years did anyone from Rome involved in the decisions that directly affected my ministry and life enter into direct dialogue with me.

In November 1985, two months after the convention, I was called in by my provincial, Father Joseph Novak, and informed that because of complaints from the local hierarchy, Cardinal Ratzinger of the Congregation for the Doc-

trine of the Faith had called in the General of the Society of
Jesus and given him an order which he was to pass on to
me, namely, that I was to "withdraw from any and all
ministry to homosexual persons." Father General Peter
Hans Kolvenbach expressed a willingness to allow me to
continue my private ministry of psychotherapy, for which
he expressed "a sincere respect and value." However, he
absolutely forbade me to take part in any way in public
ministry to gay people. I was not to be associated in any
way with homosexual causes, including passive attendance at a meeting or liturgy. He also made it clear that if
my private ministry of psychotherapy came to public
attention, he could not guarantee that the Congregation
would agree to my continuing even that. After several
months of prayer and reflection I finally sent the following reply to my provincial:

> 28 March 1986
> Good Friday
> Abbey of Gethsemani
> Trappist, Kentucky

Rev. Joseph A. Novak, S.J.
Provincial's Office
501 East Fordham Road
Bronx, New York

Dear Joe: Peace of Christ
    At our last meeting I shared with you my letter of
the 23rd of December 1985 addressed to Father General Peter Hans Kolvenbach giving my version of the
history of my relation to the Congregation for the Doctrine of the Faith as well as to my Jesuit superiors concerning my ministry to gay people. The conclusion I
reached at that time was that I could not in conscience
renounce my public ministry to my lesbian sisters and

gay brothers. You warned me of the consequences of that decision and asked me to live with the order from Father General for three months while I prayed, consulted and attempted to discern the will of God. Those three months come to an end on Tuesday, the 1st of April. I am writing to let you know that the decision remains the same. I believe that God has called me to a ministry of compassion to gay people and I cannot in conscience renounce that ministry.

I have spent the last several months since I was informed of the order of the Congregation in almost continual prayer and pain because of the need to make this decision. I have kept my promise to you not to speak out in public on homosexual issues and to forego all ministry for that three-month period. At times this was very difficult because of the extreme provocation of the all-out political attack on gay rights by the local Catholic church and the deafening silence of any "official" voice confronting that injustice. I have spent the last few days of these three months, which correspond to Holy Week, at the Abbey of Gethsemani in prayer and consultation seeking to know what God wants of me.

I have given serious consideration to your advice to me, Joe, to accept the order in a spirit of obedience, offer up the suffering that would be involved for the good of my gay family, and await eventually vindication in God's good time when I would rise like "phoenix from the ashes." This was exactly the same advice I received from the previous provincial, Father Eamon Taylor, ten years ago when I was first ordered to silence by the Congregation. At that time I accepted that advice and did my best to follow it out in a spirit of obedience for the past ten years.

I agreed to that order of silence because at the time I judged that to obey was the best way to show my love both for the Church and for my gay family. This time around, however, there is an essential difference.

Prior commands left me free to minister to my gay family. But this command orders me to give up all public ministry to gay persons. Whenever I pray over the possibility of obeying this order my spirit is troubled and I have a strong feeling that I do not have the right in conscience to abandon the gay community which has turned to me for help and guidance.

In the course of these last ten years my understanding of how I should discern the will of God has changed, I hope, for the better; it has grown and matured under the constant pressure of trying to do God's will within the confines of the restrictive directives from Rome. I believe that you and others have seen my efforts to interpret the restrictions on my freedom in the narrowest possible way as too "legalistic" an attitude and playing games with obedience. I saw those efforts as an honest attempt to try to put together my obedience to the orders I received from Rome with my obedience to the will of God calling me to a ministry of compassion to gay people.

As Eduard Schillebeeckx observes in his book *Ministry: Leadership in the Community of Jesus Christ*, "Christian obedience is also listening so as to be involved in the *kairos* of the moment of grace of a particular time, listening in obedience to the suffering of human beings and the seeds of a Christian community, and then performing specific actions in conformity with that 'voice of God.' This is also and above all a fundamental form of Christian obedience, derived from the authority of human beings who are suffering and in need." Schillebeeckx goes on to observe that where this form of obedience comes into conflict with obedience to authority, Thomas Aquinas allows that a human's conscience which has been tested in such a conflict (and not just because it is sure of itself) is free to make a decision contrary to authority and moreover adds that a conscientious person *must* do this "even if he knows that as a result he can be excommunicated by the Church."

God has granted me that grace; an intimate awareness of the suffering and the seeds of community
among my gay brothers and lesbian sisters. First of all
I had to deal with my own sufferings over the past 60
years as a gay man and then as a gay priest and religious struggling to reconcile my faith and trust in God
with my own self-acceptance. And now for the past
twenty years God has called me to a ministry to gay
people; a ministry, by the way, officially approved by
Father General Pedro Arrupe. That ministry included
my work as a psychotherapist with hundreds of gay clients. In fact I sought my training as a therapist late in
life after the closing of Woodstock Seminary and my
exclusion from teaching precisely because I wanted to
bring Christ's healing power in a professional way to
my fellow gay men and women. These past ten years
of work as a therapist with gay people have put me in
intimate contact with the special psychological pain
most gay people suffer in our culture and especially in
the Catholic Church. I became intensely aware that,
unless we are dealing with a sadistic God, what is destructive psychologically for so many people has to be
bad theology!

My ministry also included hundreds of retreats and
workshops given at retreat centers and local Dignity
chapters all over the United States and Canada that
have brought me into intimate contact with thousands
of gay people struggling to integrate a healthy self-acceptance with their love of God and neighbor. It has
been a ministry of preaching and liturgical celebration
where the extraordinary outpouring of grace and the
healing presence of the Holy Spirit were frequently
palpable.

Consequently, I am particularly aware of the great
suffering going on at present in the gay community at
large. Truly a massive crucifixion is going on in the
form of a serious plague, rivaling in its virulence any
plague of the Middle Ages, a plague that according to

experts threatens the life of one out of two gay persons, a plague that frequently leads to a lingering death with terrible pain and disfigurement. And amid all this suffering there is a mass hysteria and fear that lead to persecution and hideous injustice by the community at large. Whatever special gifts God has given me, gifts of understanding, self-acceptance and confidence in God's love and mercy, I believe that God has given them to me so that I can share them with others like myself. I have become an instrument of God's compassion.

Although I still believe, as I wrote earlier, that I am being punished unjustly for disobeying an order I never received, I hope with God's grace that I will not bear a grudge. I am sure that both you and Father Kolvenbach have prayed about this, conferred with your consultors and have reached your decision in the light of what you see as the best interest of the Society of Jesus and the Church. I am also aware that my decision can be wrong, that subtle forms of egoism and self-deceit may influence it. I am also aware, however, that fear and the urge to be secure within the Church and the Society must not deter me from bearing witness within the Church to what I think and feel is the truth. I trust that if and to the extent that I am wrong God will make that known to me and the Holy Spirit will protect those whom my error may endanger. However if my decision is right that will be proven by the good consequences that flow from it in the lives of those to whom I minister as well as in the Society of Jesus and in the Church as a whole.

I have frequently preached to my gay family that we must be prepared to "embrace ourselves as exiles"; we must be prepared to accept our exile state both within society and the Church. We must grieve and gradually let go of the desire to "belong" to all the institutions of this world. We must deepen our spiritual roots and our realization that, in direct proportion to our exiled status in this world, we belong on a deeper and more cosmic level to a community bound together by God's love and mercy. I suspect that because of my decision to continue my public ministry I must learn now to practice what I have been preaching on an ever more profound level.

I know that the imminent possibility of my separation from the Society of Jesus and from the official priesthood has caused me intense grief and sorrow; this has been my central identity for the last forty years. Yet God in her mercy has granted me some consolation. I feel sure that God's mysterious providence is guiding all our deliberations, even if their conclusions are momentarily in conflict. Someday we will both look back in joy and wonder on how God's love achieved its goal both because of and despite all of us.

Please keep me and my ministry to the gay community in your prayers, Joe, and I will continue to pray for you and the Society which I love. In obedience to the will of God as I understand it, I remain sincerely yours,

John J. McNeill, S.J.

The decision to refuse as a matter of conscience to obey the most recent order I had received from the Vatican to give up all public gay ministry brought with it a rather surprising grace of real peace and joy. I had struggled for nine years trying to discern whether my silence was following the will of God according to my vow as a Jesuit, or rather cowardice and fear of the consequences of disobedience. On the other hand, would my decision to speak out and disobey my orders be a question of pure egoism and a desire to be in the limelight? Or, again, was God calling me to speak out and accept the consequence of being separated from my religious family and from my legal right to exercise the priesthood?

Two exterior factors were influential in leading me to the decision to speak out. One was the AIDS crisis and the other was the growing homophobic reaction of my Church's hierarchy to gay people. I became convinced that gay people needed a spokesperson and defender in the Catholic Church who could speak the truth fearlessly about gayness from personal experience.

Finally, on October 19, Father Peter Hans Kolvenbach, the Superior General of the Society of Jesus, held a two-hour meeting with me in New York City. At that meeting he made it clear to me that my public ministry to gay people was not compatible with the mission of the Society of Jesus. What I understood by that was that it would come into conflict with our special fourth vow of direct obedience to the Roman Pontiff. Consequently, if I made the decision to continue in that ministry he would be obliged to expel me from the Society of Jesus. I made it clear to him from my side that I felt obliged in conscience to continue that ministry. The General assured me that my expulsion would not be a judgment on my ministry; mine would be an honorable discharge. He mentioned that Mother Teresa was expelled from her teaching order because her work in the streets of Calcutta was not compatible with the mission of her order.

The final event that precipitated my choice to renew my public ministry was the Vatican Halloween letter on homosexuality issued on 31 October 1986. I truly see the providence of God in that letter. Its homophobic spirit, in total contradiction to the spirit of the Gospels, is so obvious that no one living out the spirit of Christ can grant it any credibility or authority. I believe that in the long run it will actually help gay Catholics and other Christians to mature, stop depending on outside authority, and take charge of their own liberation. To quote a famous liberation theologian: "Liberation from oppression is a true value of the gospel. We must become aware that Christian freedom comes from within through the Spirit of Christ and we must become aware that freedom is something to be claimed, not granted from without. We must listen to the spirit within us, listen to the voice of the oppressed around us and, then, act for human rights and equality."

The Congregation's letter went far beyond any legitimate affirmation of religious or moral concern about homosexual activity. When it asserts that homosexual orientation is an "objective disorder" without taking into account all the scientific evidence that casts doubts on that opinion; when it accuses all of us who seek civil justice for gay people as being "callous" to the risk of the lives of our gay brothers and sisters because of the AIDS crisis; and, finally, when it lays blame for the "irrational and violent reactions" of homophobes on the victims of that violence because they have the effrontery to seek justice and their civil rights, the Vatican exhibits a mean and cruel spirit that is in essential conflict with both the spirit and the letter of the Gospels. I could not continue my silence in the face of that evil.

On All Soul's Day, 2 November 1986, I issued a press release in response to that letter, which broke my ten-year silence and set in motion the process of my dismissal from the Jesuits. My provincial immediately issued an order of separation and applied to the Congregation for Religious in Rome for a decree of dismissal. When that decree arrived I issued the following press release:

> After thirty-eight wonderful years as a Jesuit priest, I was informed Wednesday, 28 January 1987, that I have been dismissed from the Jesuit order by a decree issued by Jerome Hamer, Cardinal prefect for the Vatican Congregation for Religious.
>
> The grounds for my dismissal was my public dissent from the Church's teaching on homosexuality. The Vatican perceives that dissent as causing grave scandal, as injurious to the teaching authority of the Church and potentially as injurious to the salvation of souls.

I was given ten days to seek a revocation of the decree. To help me present evidence to the Vatican that
the charges against me are not true, I am calling on all
those who read my book, *The Church and the Homosexual* and/or those who have been influenced by my
ministry to write to Jerome Cardinal Hamer, O.P., Pre-
fect for the Congregation for Religious, and give witness to the influence my writings and/or my ministry
has had on their faith and their relationship to the
Church.

I do not have great hope that the decree of dismissal
will be recalled. However I am still a priest and a loyal
Catholic. I will continue my ministry to gay people
through writing, speaking and psychotherapy to the
best of my ability. And I shall always be a Jesuit in
spirit and feel a special bond of love and respect for
the Society of Jesus.

Since my decision to speak out, I have received hundreds of letters, many from clergy and religious, who have
given witness to the rightness of my decision. Many acknowledged that their return to the practice of their faith or
their priestly or religious vocation was due to my writings
and ministry. I have given dozens of newspaper interviews
and made several TV appearances, including two on the
"Phil Donahue Show" and appearances on French, Italian,
British, and Australian television. My Jesuit community
also issued a press release deploring the decision to dismiss
me from the order and expressing their admiration for my
work and their continued solidarity with me.

The final decree of dismissal was issued on 13 April
1987. In it Cardinal Hamer acknowledges the receipt of
hundreds of letters from gay people "attesting to the ben-
efits that have come to them through you. Their testimony
does not, however, alter the facts on which this dismissal is
based. Neither they nor you have denied those facts.

Certainly we are aware," Cardinal Hamer wrote, "of your deep concern for the problems and the sufferings of homosexual men and women and of your desire to alleviate that pain. However, we regret that you have sought and continue to seek remedies and solutions which are not in keeping with the authentic teaching of the Church and are, in fact, contradictory to that teaching. The Church has tried in various ways to respond to the real anguish and pain of persons of homosexual orientation. But solutions which deny the clear and constant teaching of the Church or hold out an unrealizable expectation of change in that teaching can create an illusory relief and an even greater pain and frustration." The cardinal reaffirmed the decree of dismissal and closed off all avenues of appeal.

In a recent note Walter Wink, the biblical theologian, wrote me these words: "John, when the Vatican imprudently slammed the door on you, the gust of wind it set off blew open hundreds of doors. In the craftiness of God, I swear, your impact will be increased exponentially." I will, then, continue to write and speak. I am at present at work on a book on gay spirituality entitled *Taking a Chance on God: Spiritual Messages to a Gay Christian.* It continues to be my hope and my prayer that eventually the Catholic Church will see the inadequacy of its teaching on homosexuality and the grave harm it is doing to a multitude of persons and with due humility change that teaching to conform to the will of God expressed in the lived experience of gay people themselves.

John J. McNeill
Starlight Lake, Pa.
7 July 1987

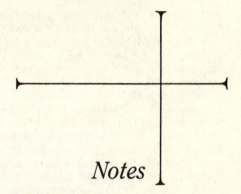

Notes

Introduction: The Need for a Reappraisal

1. Unless otherwise indicated, the word homosexual, as used in this text, includes both lesbians and gay men.

2. For a recent restatement of these traditional aims, see "Principles to Guide Confessors in Questions of Homosexuality," *Bishops' Committee on Pastoral Research and Practice*, National Conference of Catholic Bishops, 1973.

3. *A New Catechism: Catholic Faith for Adults* (New York: Herder, 1969), 384.

4. Joseph McCaffrey, "Homosexuality, Aquinas and the Church," *Catholic World* 212, no. 1 (June 1971).

5. Tom Driver, "Homosexuality: The Contemporary and Christian Contexts," *Commonweal* 98, no. 5.

6. "The Church and the Homosexual," editorial, *National Catholic Reporter* 9, no. 38.

7. Among John Harvey's more recent publications are the following: "The Controversy concerning the Psychology and Morality of Homosexuality," *American Ecclesiastical Review* 167, no. 9 (November 1973):602–29; "Attitudes of a Catholic Priest towards Homosexuality," *Bulletin of the National Guild of Catholic Psychiatrists* (December 1972):52–58.

8. John J. McNeill, *The Blondelian Synthesis: A Study of the Influence of German Philosophical Sources on Blondel's Method*

and Thought, vol. 1 in the series Studies in the History of Christian Thought, ed. Heiko Oberman (Leyden: Brill, 1966).

9. John J. McNeill, "Necessary Structures of Freedom," *Proceedings of the Jesuit Philosophical Association,* 1968. I call attention particularly to the responses to the questions and critical comments at the end of the article.

10. John J. McNeill, "Freedom of Conscience in Theological Perspective," in *Conscience: Its Freedom and Limitation* (New York: Fordham University Press, 1971), 107–24.

11. John J. McNeill, "Human Freedom and the Future," *Theological Studies* 33, no. 3 (September 1972):503–30.

12. See also the critical response of my peers Charles Curran (below, p. 30) and John Milhaven (below, chap. 5, n. 26).

13. O'Neil and Donovan, *Sexuality and Moral Responsibility* (Washington, D.C.: Catholic University Press).

14. Since the original publication of this book, there have been many excellent theological and moral studies of homosexuality and sexuality in general. Among them I include *Human Sexuality: New Directions in American Catholic Thought,* a study commissioned by the Catholic Theological Society of America and edited by Anthony Kosnik (Mahwah, N.J.: Paulist Press, 1977), and the collection of articles *A Challenge to Love: Gay and Lesbian Catholics in the Church,* edited by Robert Nugent (New York: Crossroad Publishing, 1983). Two excellent works on sexuality and Christian theology are *Embodiment* (Minneapolis: Augsburg Publishing House, 1978) and *Between Two Gardens: Reflections on Sexuality and Religious Experience* (New York: Pilgrim Press, 1983), both by James Nelson. For a lesbian perspective, I recommend Carter Heyward's *Our Passion for Justice: Images of Power, Sexuality and Liberation* (New York: Pilgrim Press, 1984).

15. Examples of these data are to be found in the sociological study of Drs. Martin S. Weinberg and Colin J. Williams, *Male Homosexuals: Their Problems and Adaptations* (New York: Oxford University Press, 1974).

Chapter 1: Moral Theology and Homosexuality

1. Charles Curran, *Catholic Moral Theology in Dialogue* (Notre Dame, Ind.: Notre Dame University Press, 1971), 184–219.

2. John J. McNeill, "The Christian Male Homosexual," *Homiletic and Pastoral Review* 70 (1970):667–77, 747–58, 828–36.

3. Curran, *Catholic Moral Theology in Dialogue*, 217.

4. Ibid., 216–17.

5. Ibid., 185–86.

6. Ibid., 219.

7. Ibid.

8. I believe the most radical difference in the approach to moral evaluation of homosexuality between Charles Curran and myself is that, as I understand it, he is still working within a natural law context which allows him to make such theoretical distinctions as "objective" versus "subjective" sin. Whereas in contrast I am approaching the problem from a personalist philosophical perspective where such a distinction would be meaningless.

9. Joseph Epstein, "Homo/Hetero: The Struggle for Sexual Identity," *Harper's*, September 1970.

10. Curran, *Catholic Moral Theology in Dialogue*, 217.

11. Dennis Altman, *Homosexual Oppression and Liberation* (New York: Dutton, 1971), 4.

12. Compiled by Harold I. Lief, *Medical Aspects of Human Sexuality* (Baltimore: Williams & Wilkins, 1975), 176. See also Eugene C. Kennedy, *The New Sexuality: Myths, Fables and Hang-Ups* (Garden City, N.Y.: Doubleday, 1972), 177–78.

13. Curran, *Catholic Moral Theology in Dialogue*, 214–16.

14. McNeill, "The Christian Male Homosexual," 828–36.

Chapter 2: Scripture and Homosexuality

1. Charles Curran, *Catholic Moral Theology in Dialogue* (Notre Dame, Ind.: Notre Dame University Press, 1971), 214–16. Since the original publication of this book, two excellent scholarly works on the treatment of homosexuality in Scripture have appeared: Robin Scrogg's *The New Testament and Homosexuality* (Philadelphia: Fortress Press, 1984) and George Edward's *Gay/Lesbian Liberation: A Biblical Perspective* (New York: Pilgrim Press, 1984).

2. Curran, *Catholic Moral Theology in Dialogue*, 214–16.

3. D. Sherwin Bailey, *Homosexuality and the Western Christian Tradition* (New York: Longmans, 1955), 1–28.

4. Curran, *Catholic Moral Theology in Dialogue*, 189.

5. Helmut Thielicke, *The Ethics of Sex* (New York: Harper, 1967), 227–84.

6. Curran, *Catholic Moral Theology in Dialogue*, 189.

7. Ibid.

8. *The Documents of Vatican II*, ed. Walter M. Abbott, S.J. (New York: America Press, 1966).

9. Alfred Kinsey et al., "Homosexual Outlet," *The Homosexual Dialectic* (Englewood Cliffs, N.J.: Prentice-Hall, 1972), 3–30.

10. Bailey, *Homosexuality and the Western Christian Tradition*, x.

11. Donald W. Cory, *The Homosexual in America* (New York: Julian Press, 1951), 8.

12. *A New Catechism: Catholic Faith for Adults* (New York: Herder, 1967), 384–85.

13. John Cavanaugh, *Counseling the Invert* (Milwaukee: Bruce, 1960), 17.

14. Quoted by Altman, *Homosexual Oppression and Liberation* (New York: Dutton, 1971), 20.

15. Bailey, *Homosexuality and the Western Christian Tradition*, 10.

16. Ibid., "Sodom and Gomorrah," 1–28.

17. "Sodomy," *Encyclopedia of Religion and Ethics*, 11:672a.

18. *Metamorph.* viii.625ff.

19. Unless otherwise indicated all scriptural excerpts are taken from *The Complete Bible: An American Translation*, trans. J. M. Powis Smith and Edgar J. Goodspeed (Chicago: University of Chicago Press, 1939).

20. There are six references to the sin of the Sodomites in the Old Testament: Gen. 13:3; 18:20; Jer. 23:19; Ezek. 16:49–50; Wis. 10:8; 19:13–14; Eccles. 16:8.

21. John McKenzie, *The World of the Judges* (Englewood Cliffs, N.J.: Prentice-Hall, 1965), 168.

22. Peter Ellis, *The Yahwist: The Bible's First Theologian* (Notre Dame, Ind.: Notre Dame University Press, 1968), 143.

23. Ibid., 199.

24. Ibid.

25. John E. Boswell, *Christianity, Social Tolerance, and Homosexuality: Gay People in Western Europe from the Beginning of the Christian Era to the Fourteenth Century* (Chicago and London: University of Chicago Press, 1980), 91–117.

26. Bailey, *Homosexuality and the Western Christian Tradition*, 39. The recently revised version has changed the translation.

27. S. Wibbing, "Die Dualistische Struktur der Paulinischen Teugend und Lasterkataloge," *Die Teugend und Lasterkataloge im Neuen Testament* (Berlin, 1959), 108–114.

28. Contrary to the popular misconception that homosexuals are effeminate, the majority of male homosexuals prefer manliness in themselves and in their partners. Further, most transvestites and males with effeminate characteristics are as a matter of fact heterosexually inclined.

29. "Thus it was natural, your majesty, for men to imitate all these things, and to become adulterers and mad after man [*arrenomaneis*], and perpetrators of other frightful deeds, in imitation of their gods (ix).

"Is it at all possible, then, for a god to be an adulterer, or a corrupter of boys [*androbatēs*], or a parricide? . . . If, indeed, the laws are just, then their gods are altogether unjust, since they commit crimes, internecine murders, sorcery, adultery, theft and *arsenokoitias*." *Arsenokoitias* is linked by the context with *arrenomaneis* in such a way that it seems likely that the author implies much more than merely homosexual practices.

30. *Patrologia Graeca,* ed. J. P. Migne, 88, 1893c (hereafter cited as *PG*): "And an inquiry concerning *arsenokoitias:* There are three kinds of this. For it is one thing to suffer it from someone else, doing which is less serious. It is yet another thing to do it to someone else, more serious than to suffer it. Another thing to suffer it from someone and do it to someone, which is even more serious than the two types already mentioned."

31. *PG* 83, 1895a: "And many even practice the vice of *arsenokoitias* with their wives."

32. Boswell, *Christianity, Social Tolerance, and Homosexuality,* 110.

33. Robert W. Wood. "Homosexual Behavior in the Bible," *Homophile Studies: One Institute Quarterly* (Winter 1962).

34. J. Edgar Brun, "Old Testament History and the Development of a Sexual Ethic," *The New Morality* (Philadelphia: Westminster).

35. Ibid.

36. Herman A. M. J. M. van de Spijker, *Die Gleichgeschlechtliche Zuneigung* (Freiburg, 1968), 94–95.

37. Neal Secor, "A Brief for a New Homosexual Ethics," *The Same Sex* (Philadelphia: Pilgrim Press, 1969), 67–70.
38. H. L. Strack and P. Billerbeck, *Kommentar zum Neuen Testament aus Talmud und Midrash* 2, 373.
39. Curran, *Catholic Moral Theology in Dialogue*, 202.
40. Karl Barth, *Church Dogmatics: A Selection,* ed. G. W. Bromily (New York: Harper, 1962), 200.
41. T. C. DeKruijf, *The Bible on Sexuality* (DePere, Wis.: St. Norbert's Abbey Press, 1966), 53. DeKruijf himself does not refer to the possibility of homosexual love. I am responsible for the application of DeKruijf's insight to the question of homosexuality.
42. Ibid., 67–69.
43. Ibid., 69. Part of the reason why marriage is no longer stressed is, as we shall see, eschatological: the expectation of the imminent end of the world and the second coming of Christ.
44. *Revised Standard Version and the Apocrypha,* copyrighted 1957 by the Division of Christian Education, National Council of the Churches of Christ in the U.S.A.
45. Ibid.
46. Evelyn Hooker, "Foundations for Christian Family Policy," *New York Council of Churches Report* (New York, 1961). Also Michael Shofield, *Sociological Aspects of Homosexuality* (Boston: Little, Brown).
47. Once again I call the attention of my readers to both the majority opinion of theologians and the tradition underlying the Church's official teaching on sexual ethics, namely, that there is a biblical norm for the ethical use of sexuality according to God's will and that norm is heterosexuality. My conclusion here is in conflict with that majority opinion and tradition. Consequently it should be carefully and critically appraised by the reader. The value of my conclusions does not rest on any authority but on the value of the reasoning and evidence that I have provided and also on the extent to which my conclusions receive confirmation in the experience of the reader.

Chapter 3: Tradition and Homosexuality

1. Charles Curran, *Catholic Moral Theology in Dialogue* (Notre Dame, Ind., Notre Dame University Press, 1971), 202.
2. Ibid., 203.

3. Citations are derived from D. Sherwin Bailey's "Homosexual Interpretation of the Sin of Sodom," *Homosexuality and the Western Christian Tradition* (New York: Longmans, 1955), 9–28.

4. W. R. Morfill and R. H. Charles, *The Book of the Secrets of Enoch* (Oxford, 1896), pp. XXIII–XXIV and 49n.

5. *De Abrahamo* xxvi.134–36; in Philo's *Works,* trans. F. H. Colson, Loeb Classical Library (Cambridge, Mass.: Harvard), 6:69–71.

6. *Gen. Rabbah* 50.7.

7. *Paed.* iii.8.

8. *Ad pop. Antioch. hom.* xix.7.

9. *De civ. Dei* xvi.30.

10. *Const. apost.* vii.2. For other references to the sin of Sodom cf. Ephraim the Syrian, *Hymns on the Faith* i.26; *Hymns on the Nativity* i; John Chrysostom, *In Heli. et vid.* iv; *De perf. carit.* vii; *In Matt. hom.* xlii.3; *In epist. ad Rom.* iv; *In epist. ad Thess.* viii.3; *In epist. ad Tit. hom.* v.4; Augustine, *De mend.* vii (10); *Contra mend.* ix (20,22); xvii (34); *Conf.* iii.15; *De fid., spe et carit.* lxxx; Gregory, *Dial.* iv.37; *Moral.* xiv.19; *Const. apost.* vi.27–28; Tertullian (?), *Sodoma.*

11. Herman A. M. J. M. van de Spijker, *Die Gleichgeschlechtliche Zuneigung* (Freiburg, 1968), 100–101.

12. *Inst.* iv; xviii.4. The research materials for the development of law are derived from Bailey's *Homosexuality and the Western Christian Tradition.*

13. *Cod. Theod.* ix; vii.3 (*Cod. Just.* ix; ix.31), *The Theodosian Code,* trans. Clyde Pharr (Princeton: Princeton University Press, 1952), 231–32.

14. W. G. Holmes, *The Age of Justinian and Theodora* (London, 1921), 1:121.

15. *Cod. Theod.* ix; vii.6; cf. Pharr, *The Theodosian Code,* 232.

16. *Cod. Justin.* nov. 77.

17. *Cod. Justin.* nov. 141.

18. William Blackstone, *Commentary on the Laws of England,* ed. J. Chitty (London, 1826), 4:215.

19. *Conc. Illib.* 71.

20. *Conc. Ancyr.* 16, 17. Cf. C. H. Turner, *Ecclesiae Occidentales Monumenta Juris Antiquissima* (Oxford, 1909), 11:19. For the influence of this council on future enactments see *Capit. Aquisgran* (789) 48, Mansi xviib, col. 230; *Capit. Carol. mag.* 48,

Mansi xviib, col. 710; *Capit. Carol. mag. et Ludovic.* 82, Mansi
xviib, col. 839; *Canones Isaac episc. Lingonen* 4, 11, Mansi xviib,
col. 1259; *Conc. Paris* (829) 1, 34, Mansi xiv, col. 560.

21. *Epist.* ccxvii (*ad Amphiloch.*), can. 62.

22. *Epist. canonica* iv.

23. *Conc. Tolitan.* 16, 3, Mansi xii, col. 71.

24. *Conc. Neapol.* 8, Mansi xxi, cols. 261–64.

25. Cf. *Synod. constit. Odo. episc. Paris* (ca. 1196) 4, 5 (the
pope or the bishop), Mansi xxiii, col. 678; *Conc. Prov. Fritzlar*
(1246) 4 (bishop), Mansi xxiii, col. 726; *Stat. syn. eccl. Leod.* (1287)
4 (bishop), Mansi xxiv, col. 891; *Conc. Ramense.* (1408), Mansi
xxvi, col. 1073.

26. *Patrologia Latina,* ed. J. P. Migne, 145, col. 161 (hereafter
cited as *PL*).

27. Mansi xix, cols. 685–86.

28. *Chron.* in Rolls series, ed. W. Stubbs (London, 1879), vol.
2, under A.D. 1120.

29. Bailey, *Homosexuality and the Western Christian Tradition,* 135–44.

30. Louis Crompton, "Module No. 10; Gay Genocide: From
Leviticus to Hitler," *Salvatorian Justice and Peace Commission:
Gay Minority Task Force.* See also Wolfgang Harthauser, "Der
Massenmord an Homosexuellen im Dritten Reich," *Der Grosse
Tabu,* ed. William S. Schlegel (Munich: Rütten & Leening Verlag,
1967).

31. Neale Secor, *The Same Sex* (Philadelphia: Pilgrim Press,
1969), 71.

32. G. Rattray Taylor, *Sex in History* (New York: Vanguard
Press, 1954), chap. 4, pp. 72ff.

33. The most recent repetition of the legal tradition was the
Supreme Court decision in 1986 upholding the sodomy laws of the
state of Georgia because of "millennia of moral judgment" based
on the Sodom and Gomorrah myth.

34. Bailey, *Homosexuality and the Western Christian Tradition,* 161–62.

35. *Paed.* 10.

36. *De fac. nat.* 1.6.

37. Bailey, *Homosexuality and the Western Christian Tradition,* 164.

38. George Weinberg, *Society and the Healthy Homosexual*
(New York: St. Martin's Press, 1972), 1–21.

39. John Harvey, "Homosexuality as a Pastoral Problem," *Theological Studies* 16 (1955):86–108.

40. Bailey, *Homosexuality and the Western Christian Tradition*, 162.

Chapter 4: Tradition and Human Nature

1. *Const. Apost.* vi.11; vi.28.
2. *De pudic.* iv.
3. *In Epist. ad Rom.* iv.
4. Michel Spanneut, *Le Stoicisme des pères de l'église de Clement de Rome à Clement d'Alexandrie* (Paris, 1957), 432.
5. See F. Copleston, *A History of Philosophy*, vol. 1, pt. 2 (Garden City, N.Y.: Doubleday, 1962), 138ff.
6. *Diogenes Laertius* 7.86ff.
7. Marcus Aurelius, *Med.* 5.27.
8. See "Stoicism," *New Catholic Encyclopedia*, 716–21.
9. Ibid., 720.
10. *Paed.* 1, chap. 13.
11. Marcus Aurelius, *Med.* 7.29.
12. Ibid., 19.
13. Seneca, *Epist.* 120, 14; 65, 16.
14. Aquinas, *Commentary on the Nichomachean Ethics*, trans. C. I. Litzinger (Chicago: Regnery, 1964), vol. 2, bk. 9, lect. 10, no. 1896.
15. Von Arnim, *Stoic. Vet. Frag.*, 1:59–60.
16. Emil Brunner, *The Divine Imperative* (Philadelphia: Westminster, 1947), 364.
17. *On the Generation of Animals*, 737a.
18. *The City of God* 14.26. See also *On Marriage and Concupiscence* 2.5.
19. *"De divisione naturae,"* PL 122, 57c.
20. *Paed.* 2.10; *De concept.* 92.2.
21. *I Apol.* 29.1.
22. *In Evang. Luc.* 17.29.
23. *Summa Theol.* II-II, q. 153, 3.
24. Ibid., III, q. 32, 4.
25. Ibid., I, q. 99, 2.
26. Ibid., I, q. 92, 1.
27. Ibid., I, q. 98.

28. See Joseph McCaffrey, "Homosexuality, Aquinas and the Church," *Catholic World* 212, no. 1 (July 1971).

29. *Summa Theol.* II-II, q. 154, 12, ad 1.

30. Ibid., I-II, q. 37, 7.

31. Charles Curran, *Catholic Moral Theology in Dialogue* (Notre Dame, Ind.: Notre Dame University Press, 1971), 199.

32. Ibid., 204.

33. Ibid.

34. See *Seven Great Encyclicals* (Paramus, N.J.: Paulist Press, 1963), 93–94.

35. Ibid., 84.

36. "Pastoral Constitution on the Church in the Modern World—a Response," *The Documents of Vatican II,* ed. W. Abbott, 314–15. See also "The Pastoral Constitution . . ." no. 50: "Marriage to be sure is not instituted solely for procreation. Rather, its very nature as an unbreakable compact between persons, and the welfare of the children, both demand that the mutual love of the spouses, too, be embodied in a rightly ordered manner, that it grow and ripen. Therefore, marriage persists as a whole manner and communion of life, and maintains its value and indissolubility, even when offspring are lacking—despite, rather often, the very intense desire of the couple."

37. Søren Kierkegaard, *Fear and Trembling* (Garden City, N.Y.: Doubleday, 1941), 80–82.

38. See John J. McNeill, "Freedom and the Future," *Theological Studies* 33, no. 3 (September 1972):503–30.

39. Tom Driver, *Sex: Thoughts for Contemporary Christians* (Garden City, N.Y.: Doubleday, 1972), 49–62.

40. For evidence on this point see Wainwright Churchill, *Homosexual Behavior among Males* (New York: Hawthorn Books, 1967).

41. Paul Lehmann, *Ethics in a Christian Context* (London: SCM, 1963), 136.

42. H. Kimball-Jones, *Toward a Christian Understanding of Homosexuality* (New York: Association Press, 1966), 56.

43. T. C. DeKruijf, *The Bible on Sexuality* (DePere, Wis.: St. Norbert's Abbey Press, 1966), 69.

Chapter 5: The Human Sciences and Homosexuality

1. Charles Curran, *Catholic Moral Theology in Dialogue* (Notre Dame, Ind.: Notre Dame University Press, 1971), 190.

2. Ibid., 192. See also John Giles Milhaven, *Toward a New Catholic Morality* (New York: Doubleday, 1972), 59–63.

3. Curran, *Catholic Moral Theology in Dialogue*, 193.

4. Ibid.

5. Ibid., 203.

6. Ibid.

7. William Simon and John Gagnon, "Homosexuality: The Formation of a Sociological Perspective," *Journal of Health and Sociological Behavior* 8 (1966):177–85.

8. Curran, *Catholic Moral Theology in Dialogue*, 196.

9. Ibid., 203.

10. Dennis Altman, *Homosexual Oppression and Liberation* (New York: Dutton, 1971), 52.

11. Edmund Bergler, *Homosexuality: Disease or Way of Life* (New York: Collier, 1956), 1–10.

12. Irving Bieber, *Homosexuality: A Psychoanalytic Study* (New York: Basic Books, 1962), 5.

13. Altman, *Homosexual Oppression and Liberation*, 44–46.

14. Bergler, *Homosexuality: Disease or Way of Life*, 4.

15. Sigmund Freud, "Letter to an American Mother," in *The Problem of Homosexuality in Modern Society*, ed. Hendrick Riutenbeek (New York: Dutton, 1963), 1–2.

16. Louis Crompton, *Homosexuality and the Sickness Theory* (San Francisco: The Society for Individual Rights, 1963), 4.

17. See Wainwright Churchill, *Homosexual Behavior among Males* (New York: Hawthorn Books, 1967), 106–22.

18. John Cavanaugh, *Counseling the Invert* (Milwaukee: Bruce, 1960), 37.

19. H. Kimball-Jones, *Toward a Christian Understanding of Homosexuality* (New York: Association Press, 1966), 52.

20. Churchill, *Homosexual Behavior among Males*, 105.

21. Ibid.

22. Evelyn Hooker, "Foundations for Christian Family Policy," *New York Council of Churches Report* (New York, 1961).

23. Kimball-Jones, *Toward a Christian Understanding of Homosexuality*. I would certainly change this judgment today. Since

the decision of the American Psychiatric Association to remove homosexuality from the category of mental disorder, many excellent studies have been done on homosexuality as a normal variant of sexual orientation. I recommend especially *Homosexual Behavior: A Modern Reappraisal*, Judd Marmor, ed. (New York: Basic Books, 1980). I also recommend *Innovations in Psychotherapy With Homosexuals*, edited by Emery Hetrick and Terry Stein (Washington, D.C.: American Psychiatric Press, 1984).

24. John Milhaven, "Homosexuality and the Christian," *Homiletic and Pastoral Review* 58, no. 8 (May 1968):665.

25. Ibid., 667–68.

26. In a letter to the editors of the *National Catholic Reporter*, John Milhaven himself announced that in the light of new evidence he rejects his former opinion: "McNeill is right. My original essay had ignored the important evidence he then set forth. In revising my essay for book publication I acknowledged McNeill's argument and evidence. I altered substantially my own position, bringing it closer to his." (See "Repartee," *National Catholic Reporter*, 4 December 1975.)

27. Bergler, *Homosexuality: Disease or Way of Life*, 24.

28. Bieber, *Homosexuality: A Psychoanalytic Study*, 100–150.

29. For a history of causes and cures as they have been pursued through time see Arno Karlen's *Sexuality and Homosexuality* (New York: Norton, 1972). For a critical summary of recent "cure" techniques of therapy see G. Weinberg, "The Case against Trying to Convert," *Society and the Healthy Homosexual* (New York: St. Martin's Press, 1972), 41–48.

30. Gerald C. Davison, President of the Association for Advancement of Behavior Therapy, recently rejected the use of aversion therapy as a means of "curing" the psychic condition of homosexuality. On the contrary, Mr. Davison reports, "the vast majority of behavior therapists would indeed help their homosexual clients adjust more satisfactorily to a permanent homosexual identity."

31. Thomas Szasz, *The Manufacture of Madness* (New York: Harper, 1970). Reprinted as "The Product Conversion: From Heresy to Illness," in *The Homosexual Dialectic*, ed. J. McCaffrey (New Jersey, 1972), 101–20.

32. Szasz, *The Homosexual Dialectic*, 108.

33. Ibid., 109.

34. Irving Bieber, *New York Times*, 15 September 1967, 27.

35. Robert Lindner, *Must You Conform?* (New York: Holt, 1956), 32–33.

36. Weinberg, *Society and the Healthy Homosexual*, 3–21.

37. Ibid., Preface.

38. Ibid., 3.

Chapter 6: Toward a Positive Approach of Moral Theology

1. Pierre-Claude Nappey, "An Open Letter on Homosexuality," in *Sex: Thoughts for Contemporary Christians*, ed. Michael Taylor (Garden City, N.Y.: Doubleday, 1972), 211.

2. Ibid., 212.

3. *New York Times*, 25 February 1972, 41.

4. Ibid.

5. Nappey, "An Open Letter on Homosexuality."

6. J. Edgar Brun, *The New Morality* (Philadelphia: Westminster).

7. Eugene Kennedy, *The New Sexuality: Myths, Fables and Hang-Ups* (Garden City, N.Y.: Doubleday, 1973), 179–80.

8. Nappey, "An Open Letter on Homosexuality," 217–18.

9. Ibid., 210, 218.

10. Kennedy, *The New Sexuality*, 179.

11. C. G. Jung, *The Collected Works*, trans. R. F. C. Hull (New York: Pantheon, 1959), vol. 9, pt. 1, 86–87.

12. Rainer Maria Rilke, *Letters to a Young Poet*, trans. M. D. Herter (New York: Norton, 1962), 58–59.

13. Louis Crompton, "Module No. 10; Gay Genocide: From Leviticus to Hitler," *Salvatorian Justice and Peace Commission: Gay Minority Task Force*. See also Wolfgang Harthauser, "Der Massenmord an Homosexuellen im Dritten Reich," in *Der Grosse Tabu*, ed. William S. Schlegel (Munich: Rütten & Leening Verlag, 1967), 17–37.

14. Dennis Altman, *Homosexual Oppression and Liberation* (New York: Dutton, 1971), 74–75.

15. Helmut Thielicke, *The Ethics of Sex* (New York: Harper, 1967), 227–84.

16. Mark Freedman, "Far from Illness: Homosexuals May Be Healthier than Straights," *Psychology Today* 8, no. 10 (March 1975):27–33.

17. G. Rattray Taylor, *Sex in History* (New York: Vanguard Press, 1954), 72ff.

18. C. G. Jung, *Collected Works* 9:86.

Chapter 7: Pastoral Ministry to the Homosexual Community

1. Paul Lehmann, *Ethics in a Christian Context* (London: SCM, 1963), 137.

2. In order to be accepted by a majority of the delegates, the final resolution had to be reworded to eliminate reference to a homosexual community as such. Consequently, it read "Christian ministry to the homosexual." Many delegates felt that the Church could not proceed to recognize the existence of a homosexual community and retain its traditional moral judgment on homosexual activities. Thus the only ministry possible would be one to individuals as such.

3. H. Kimball-Jones, *Toward a Christian Understanding of Homosexuality* (New York: Association Press, 1966), 12–13.

4. Robert Gleason and George Hagmaier, *Counseling the Catholic* (New York: Sheed and Ward, 1957), 100.

5. Gordon Westwood, *A Minority: A Report on the Life of the Male Homosexual in Great Britain* (New York: Fernhill House, 1960), 10.

6. John Cavanaugh, *Counseling the Invert* (Milwaukee: Bruce, 1960), 258–59.

7. Richard F. Hettlinger, *Living with Sex: The Student's Dilemma* (New York: Seabury, 1966), 94–112.

8. D. J. West, *Homosexuality* (London, 1960), 47.

9. Donald W. Cory and John LeRoy, *The Homosexual and His Society* (New York: Citadel, 1963), 104–5.

10. Michael Buckley, *Morality and the Homosexual* (London: Lamb's, 1959), 19.

11. Cavanaugh, *Counseling the Invert*, 262.

12. Ibid., 263.

13. Ibid., 262.

14. James Baldwin, *Nobody Knows My Name* (New York: Dial Press, 1961).

15. Gleason and Hagmaier, *Counseling the Catholic*, 102.

16. H. Kimball-Jones, *Toward a Christian Understanding of Homosexuality*, 88.

17. Westwood, *A Minority*, 28.

18. West, *Homosexuality*, 51.

19. Marcus Hirschfield, "Sublimation and the Homosexual," *Pastoral Psychology* 2, no. 18 (November 1951).

20. William Hague, "Clerical and Lay Value Systems," *Modern Society* 12, no. 4 (August 1969).

21. Cf. O'Neil and Donovan, *Sexuality and Moral Responsibility* (Washington, D.C.: Catholic University Press): "Sin is properly sin because it opposes the will of God. But this 'will of God' is neither arbitrary nor vindictive. Following the thought of Aquinas we see that the divine will is really identical with the true good of man. . . . In this context it is worthwhile to repeat our basic premise, good morality and good psychology cannot be in conflict. There is no contradiction between the supernatural good of man and his ethical good."

22. Helmut Thielicke, *The Ethics of Sex* (New York: Harper, 1967), 105.

23. *Dignity: A Monthly Newsletter for Catholic Homophiles and Concerned Heterophiles* 3, no. 4 (5 May 1972).

24. Martin S. Weinberg and Colin J. Williams, *Male Homosexuals: Their Problems and Adaptations* (New York: Oxford University Press, 1974).

25. Many excellent advances have been made in recent years toward a more inclusive attitude toward lesbians and gay men in several of the mainline churches. However, most gay Christians still feel the need of a separate church or a separate organization within the church where they can worship in safety without fear of being denounced or judged from the pulpit. The Roman Catholic Church has recently taken a step backward with regard to homosexuality. In the Halloween letter of 31 October 1986, to all the bishops of the world, the Vatican again judged homosexual orientation to be an "objective disorder" and a "tendency to evil."

26. *Journal of the New York Mission of the Metropolitan Community Church* 1, no. 1 (March 1972).

27. Information about Dignity can be obtained by writing to Dignity, Inc., 1500 Massachusetts Avenue, N.W., Suite 11, Washington, D.C., 20005; (202) 861-0017.

28. Thielicke, *The Ethics of Sex*, 281–87.

29. *Toward a Quaker View of Sex*, ed. Alastair Huron (London, 1963).

30. That there can be a morally good sexual relationship between two homosexuals who love each other is my personal conviction. Once again I call attention of my readers to the fact that this conviction contradicts the traditional teaching of the Church in this matter. It is not my intention to attempt to supplant the magisterium but, rather, to invite a public debate and discussion of this issue in the hope that the Church will listen and reconsider its position. In the meantime the only authority my conviction has is the intrinsic value of the reasoning and evidence that I can bring to its support.

31. Norman Pittenger, *Time for Consent* (London: SCM, 1970), 122–23.

32. Richard A. McCormick, "Notes on Moral Theology," *Theological Studies* 33, no. 1 (March 1972):112–13. See also Francis H. Touchet, "A View from the Other Side of the Garden," *Listening* (Winter 1971):42–48.

Chapter 8: Conclusion: Justice, the Church, and the Homosexual

1. Synod Document, 9 December 1971. Translated in *Catholic Mind* 70, no. 1261 (March 1972):53.

2. Ibid., 57.

3. Ibid., 59.

4. "The Quest for Justice: Guidelines to a Creative Response by American Catholics to the 1971 Synod Statement, 'Justice in the World'." Issued by the Jesuit Center of Concern, 25 June 1972.

5. Synod, 22 October 1971. Quoted in "The Quest for Justice," 5.

6. *Justice in the World*, 60.

7. John Cardinal Carberry, Synod, 21 October 1971. Quoted in "The Quest for Justice," 11.

8. *Justice in the World*, 55.

9. John Cardinal Dearden, Synod, 21 October 1971. Quoted in "The Quest for Justice," 4.

Appendix 2: Some Pastoral Reflections on AIDS

1. Some of these theological reflections on AIDS were originally published in a review of John E. Fortunato's book *AIDS: The Spiritual Dilemma*. The review, entitled "AIDS: A Corner of Salvation," appeared in the 3 August 1987 issue of *Christianity and Crisis* (vol. 47, no. 11), pp. 266–68.

2. John E. Fortunato, *AIDS: The Spiritual Dilemma* (San Francisco: Harper and Row, 1987).

3. Ibid., 78–79.

4. Ibid., 85–86.

Index

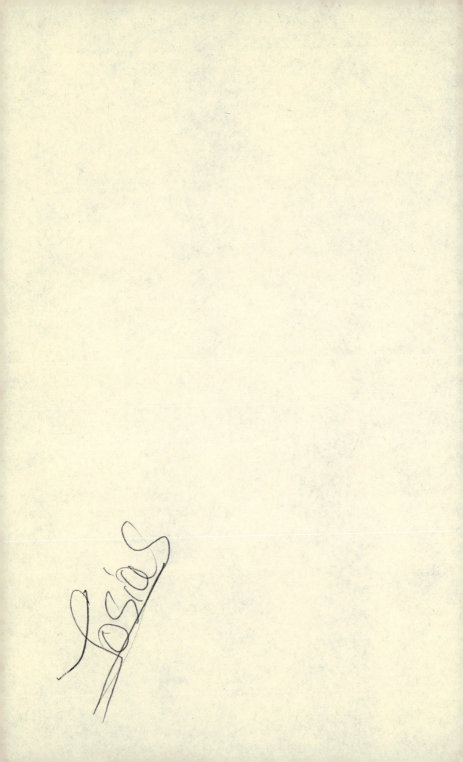